Deadbeat Dams

T0162253

Deadbeat Dams

Why We Should Abolish the
U.S. Bureau of Reclamation and
Tear Down Glen Canyon Dam

Daniel P. Beard
Former Commissioner of the U.S. Bureau of Reclamation

JOHNSON BOOKS
AN IMPRINT OF BOWER HOUSE
DENVER

Cover and text design by D.K. Luraas
Cover photos courtesy iStock

Library of Congress Cataloging-in-Publication Data
Beard, Daniel Perry, 1943-
   Deadbeat dams : why we should abolish the U.S. Bureau of Reclamation and tear down Glen Canyon Dam / Daniel P. Beard, Former Commissioner of the U.S. Bureau of Reclamation.
       pages cm
   ISBN 978-1-55566-460-2 (alk. paper)
   1. United States. Bureau of Reclamation. 2. Water supply—Government policy—West (U.S.) 3. Dams—United States. 4. Reclamation of land—Government policy—West (U.S.) I. Title.
   HD1694.A5B43 2015
   333.9100978—dc23

                                        2015001554

Printed in Canada.

9 8 7 6 5 4

*For the next generation of
water reform advocates*

Contents

Contents

Acknowledgments

When I sat down to write this book, I was filled with enthusiasm and passion to lay out my case for reform. It quickly became apparent, however, that I needed help. I needed a guiding hand to help me organize my thoughts and tell me how to engage readers. Jeff Benedict provided that helping hand. He skillfully helped me to structure the book and provided critical editorial guidance on early drafts. Thank you Jeff for your help.

This book wouldn't have been possible without the support of many people throughout a long career in government and the advocacy community. I can't thank everyone, but I do want to give special recognition to the following:

To Guy Martin and Cecil Andrus for hiring me at the Interior Department and giving me a chance to work on water reform issues. To Bruce Babbitt and John Leshy for allowing me a second chance to make a difference at the national level. To my many colleagues on the House Natural Resources Committee for their support and friendship over the past three decades. Steve Lanich and Lori Sonken were with me from the beginning, and they were joined by Dan Adamson, Jeff Petrich, Charlene Dougherty, Julie Petro Lowndes, Marie Howard, Tadd Johnson, Liz Birnbaum and Celia Boddington. To my Senate colleagues, Tom Jensen and Dana Cooper, thank you for helping to move legislation and your support over the years.

I wouldn't have been able to write this book without the support of former Congressman George Miller and his Chiefs of Staff John Lawrence and Danny Weiss. They hired me to work at the House of Representatives and gave me the freedom to take on just about any water issue and develop innovative solutions. George's passion and courage was infectious and he never shied away from a good idea just because it was controversial. John always provided calm guidance, strong support, and friendship. Danny Weiss helped get out the message, and carried on the reform tradition.

While I was Commissioner of the Bureau of Reclamation, Don Glaser, Ed Osann, Janna Sidley, Lisa Guide, and Paul Bledsoe provided me with support, friendship, and astute advice. I'm grateful.

I want to thank Steve Lanich and Dave Weiman for providing me with ideas, suggestions, factual information, and support for more than forty years. They have become good friends and essential colleagues.

This book would have remained just another unpublished manuscript had it not been for the help and insistence of Dave Wegner. He was a never-ending source of information for me. He calmly answered question after question and never grew bored when I asked him to explain something one more time. He never lost faith that this book would be published and I'm grateful to him for his persistence.

Gary Wockner breathed new life into this project. He quickly read my manuscript, provided thoughtful comments, and then insisted that it had to be published "as soon as possible." He undertook a whirlwind of activity that helped make publication possible, and I'm grateful for his help

A big thank you to my editor at Big Earth Publishing, Mira Perrizo, who believed in this project and provided deft editing and advice to a novice author.

While all these people helped make this book possible, I'm ultimately responsible for the views and opinions expressed. In many cases, my friends and colleagues would probably disagree with my recommendations, and I would welcome a debate with them. Nevertheless, these are my words, my opinions, and my recommendations. Don't blame them.

I want to thank my children Allison, Nick, and Peter, daughter-in-law Jenni and son-in-law Jim for their support and encouragement on this project. To my grandchildren Lily and Jack, thank you for giving me hope for a better future. Finally, it would have been impossible for me to write this book without the love, support, and understanding of my wife, Dana. I'm grateful for her never-ending support and encouragement on this project and in many other ventures. It has been a remarkable forty-eight years together.

Prelude

If the Taxpayers Only Knew

"What a waste, what a colossal waste. The taxpayers would be outraged if they knew what was really going on here," I thought to myself.

It was nearly ten years ago and I was sitting on the dais looking out at the people attending a meeting of the Colorado River Water Users Association. The association had gathered for their annual meeting amid the fake opulence of Caesars Palace in Las Vegas. They had asked five former commissioners of the U.S. Bureau of Reclamation, including myself, to reflect on our tenure directing the federal agency responsible for building and operating water projects across the West, such as Hoover, Glen Canyon, and Grand Coulee Dams.

This minor agency of fifty-five hundred employees had had an indelible impact on the West. By building dams and canals, the agency had provided subsidized water and electric power to farms and cities across the West for just over a hundred years. The Bureau of Reclamation had been instrumental in the growth of cities like Los Angeles, Las Vegas, and Phoenix, the development of agriculture in California's Central and Imperial Valleys, and many other parts of the West.

But there was another side to the agency's history. These projects also destroyed hundreds of miles of free-flowing rivers, promoted excessive water use, and sent billions of dollars in subsidies to a small number of people—many of whom sat in the audience at Caesars Palace. The agency had outlived whatever usefulness it had and now needed to be abolished. Some of its trademark

1

facilities, such as Glen Canyon Dam, needed to be removed to meet contemporary water needs.

I had prepared a polite set of non-controversial remarks for the event. But as I sat there observing the people in the audience and listening to the other speakers, it occurred to me that the public deserved to learn what was really going on.

I set aside my remarks and spoke from the heart. I explained that we're lavishing billions of dollars of federal taxpayer money on a small group of people who have come to think of this money as an entitlement. This arrangement is preserved by a complicit Congress and an out-of-date federal bureaucracy. Billions of gallons of water are being wasted by growing crops we don't need. We think nothing of drying up rivers, killing fish, and destroying tourism so that a hobby farmer can grow hay for his daughter's horse. We promote water waste on a massive scale under the mistaken impression that water should be treated as a "free" commodity. We're repeating failed approaches to solving problems that will have reached crisis proportions. Facilities built to meet spurious needs identified in the nineteenth and early twentieth centuries are out of date and need to be removed.

As I finished my remarks, I looked out at the crowd and there seemed to be two emotions etched on their faces. Some of the people had raised eyebrows and a "did-he-just-say-what-I-thought-he-said?" look. The rest of the crowd had deep furrowed brows, and if looks could kill, I would have been a dead man.

As I left the dais, a young lady from a water education group approached. With cynicism dripping from every word, she said: "Well, you're still as controversial as ever." I took her comment as a compliment.

When I returned from Las Vegas, I threw myself into the task of finding someone to write a book about the need to change western water policies. I wanted to expose the public to the lack of common sense, corruption, and utter waste I had witnessed over a long government career and propose a series of reforms.

Despite my best efforts, I couldn't find any takers. If someone was going to write that book, I was going to have to do it.

This certainly isn't a new subject to me. For almost forty years, I worked in a variety of professional capacities on water policy issues. I was involved in one way or another in most major western water policy debate or legislation during that period. I had been a non-profit advocate, consultant, government administrator, political appointee under two Presidents, chief of staff to a U.S. senator, and staff director for a congressional committee.

I remember thinking at a particularly boring congressional hearing I attended in the House of Representatives that I had sat in every chair in the room. I had sat in the audience, at the witness table, behind the members of Congress passing questions, and at the dais asking questions of witnesses.

But it wasn't until my emotions got the best of me in Las Vegas that I even considered writing a book on the subject. Debates about western water are the stuff of legends. Almost everyone has heard the saying attributed to Mark Twain that in the West, "Whiskey is fer drinking, and water is fer fightin'." Murders, gunfights, lawsuits, demonstrations, and ferocious political battles have all been part of western water debates. Hundreds of books have been written, thousands of websites created, and miles of column inches in newspapers have chronicled activities for over a century.

What could I say that would add to this subject?

While a great deal has been written, I had always felt that authors were pulling their punches. They weren't being completely candid with their readers. They weren't telling the real story of western water. Someone who had been on the "inside" of the system needed to expose it.

America is facing a water crisis and nowhere is this more evident than in the West where significant problems abound. At this writing, the western United States is struggling to survive a fifteen-year drought that is the worst in nearly a thousand years. One scientist called it a "megadrought." "Bathtub rings" now circle

Lake Mead, America's largest reservoir, because the lake is now half empty. Water levels in reservoirs across the West have dropped to record lows. As of August 2014, 100 percent of California was considered in a drought. Water and power shortages are now a real possibility for Las Vegas, Phoenix, Los Angeles, and other major western cities. The megadrought will start to rattle through the national economy if these trends continue, causing food prices to rise and impacting our national economy to the tune of billions of dollars.

How are we responding to this growing crisis? We're not.

Our leaders appear to be ostriches with their heads stuck in the ground. Government agencies spend millions of dollars on studies that find new ways to restate the obvious. Government officials scurry from meeting to meeting desperately searching for painless "solutions," which give the appearance of addressing problems without doing so. Politicians are in denial and everyone avoids hard choices.

None of this should surprise us. We've known the megadrought was coming for years. Scientists and even government-chartered commissions have predicted our drought "malaise." Despite bold and sometimes career-threatening predictions by some scientists, our government officials and their parasitic supplicants have squelched any effort to begin to address these problems. They have established slick public relations campaigns with alliterative titles designed to delay any effort to make a decision. The George W. Bush Administration created the "Water 2025" campaign to avoid today's problems and not be prepared for tomorrow's. The Obama Administration isn't much better. Their solution is for us to become "WaterSMART" by awarding grants to their friends and ignoring their critics.

Why can't our leaders face reality and begin to address these issues?

They're not willing to identify and tackle the root cause of the West's present water problems because we have allowed a small group of individuals and organizations, whom I refer to as the "Water Nobility," to receive billions of dollars in subsidies and to control western water policy. The Water Nobility feels it is a birthright to which they are entitled. Taxpayers should continue to take money out of their wallets and give it to the Water Nobility. They keep the public uninformed. They squelch creativity, ignore common sense, and perpetuate myths. All the while, they line their pockets with taxpayer dollars and demand even more money.

The American public should know how their tax dollars are being used to enrich this small group of western water interests. The Water Nobility is pampered and coddled by a willing Congress and federal bureaucracy. The Nobility has come to view the benefits they receive from the taxpayers as just and appropriate. If we don't force them to release their grip, the Water Nobility will continue to line their own pockets with billions of dollars in federal subsidies and payments for another fifty to a hundred years, the megadrought will continue, western rivers will continue to suffer damage, and economic progress in many regions will be threatened.

Within the last decade, a series of disturbing developments have added to the urgent need to reform this system. Not content with wasting tens of millions of tax dollars on wasteful water projects, members of Congress and state legislators are still proposing billions of dollars for new uneconomic and environmentally destructive water projects. They continue to pass legislation enriching a few people to the tune of hundreds of millions of dollars.

The megadrought in the West has grown in severity and threatens to have a national impact. Climate change is altering rainfall and precipitation patterns, and we are just now realizing that this will force us to completely re-think how we manage water resources.

A renewed effort is being made by some national politicians to attack scientists because they don't like the answers they receive on many fundamental questions, including water issues. Scientists are called on the carpet before congressional committees while other scientists are having their agencies abolished.

When I began writing this book, I thought that if people learned what was going on, they would be outraged, and that outrage would lead to reform. But I soon realized outrage by itself leads nowhere. What we need are concerned people who are armed with an agenda for reform. Outrage can lead to action, but those actions need to be channeled in the right direction.

The purpose of this book is to inform and educate people about how their tax dollars are being used and misused, why we are ignoring some immediate problems, and what can be done to correct this state of affairs.

In the pages that follow, the faults of the present system of federally assisted water management efforts will be amply detailed. But a series of specific changes will be recommended to re-direct water policy decision-making and implementation. These reforms will loosen the grip of the Water Nobility and improve the decisions made in Congress and the federal bureaucracy and states on water matters. These reforms show how we can extract the federal government from worthless activities that cost millions and provide little or no benefit. The reforms will also lay out how and why we need to get prepared for a more uncertain future.

Can one person laying out a reform agenda like this make a difference? Ten years ago, I had my doubts, but not today. A considerable amount has changed in the world of politics and public policy over the past decade. It used to be that those seeking reform were forced to write and publish a tome and hope that someone in a position of influence would read it. Maybe congressional hearings might be held. Maybe nongovernmental organizations would pick up the elements of a reform agenda and assist in marketing the effort. Maybe, maybe, maybe.

But with the rise of the Internet and social media, a single individual with a compelling agenda can make a difference. We now have the ability to target and send information to thousands of people with the stroke of a keyboard. The WikiLeaks episode and the National Security Agency disclosures of Edward Snowden aptly demonstrate what one individual can do with compelling information. No matter what the morality of these episodes, they show that information is power, and when millions of people become aware of that information, change can and does occur.

During this same period, our political ethos has also changed. The new electronic media generation and many taxpayers feel that they have a "right to know" how the system works, and what those in a position of power are doing with their tax dollars. They want to know what is being withheld from them, and they no longer have to wait for organizations or governments to blow the whistle or divulge information. Now, any individual with a smart phone or a blog is capable of shining the bright light of public opinion on outrageous practices and policies.

Creating a "buzz" or getting an idea to go "viral" is not easy. But it is possible if people know the facts and they're armed with an agenda for change. It is for this reason that I have written this book. I want to lay out the issues, and more important, lay out an agenda for reform that can be used as ammunition by a new generation of water reformers.

1

Falling Down the Rabbit Hole

*Predetermined political solutions to water problems
always trump common sense and fiscal sanity.*

When the President announces that he's nominating you to a position requiring Senate confirmation, you make appointments to introduce yourself to the senators who have an interest in the position you're being considered for.

I assumed this experience would be like most other congressional visits, where you see an aide, plead your case, and leave. Not with confirmation appointments. Senators actually *want* to meet with you. Their interest in talking one-on-one isn't driven entirely by a desire to chat with you or debate great policy issues. Most have a pet project they want to encourage you to make a priority, or they want to challenge you on a position you've taken in the past with which they disagree.

When I was nominated by President Bill Clinton to be the commissioner of the Bureau of Reclamation in 1993, I had the opportunity to meet with quite a few western senators. Predictably, most pushed their favorite project or program, but there was one meeting that permanently influenced my outlook on water issues.

Senator Pete Domenici of New Mexico was elected to the Senate in 1972 and had climbed the seniority ladder to become a leading member of the Senate Energy Committee. He was fully aware of federal water projects because those projects had provided water for cities and farms throughout his state for many years. He was even more aware of the sensitive political nature of water politics.

At the same time, as former Budget Committee chair, he often questioned the underlying rationale for key government programs, and federal water projects were no exception.

As I entered his office, he was signing letters. "While I finish these," he said, "let me ask you a question. Why do we need a Bureau of Reclamation?"

It was such a simple, profound question. Yet no one had ever asked me that before. I thought for a second. "Senator," I said, "we don't need the Bureau of Reclamation. It doesn't do anything that can't be done by another government agency or the private sector. However, let me ask you something. Would you like to be known as the senator who got rid of the Bureau?"

He stopped signing letters, looked up at me, smiled, and said, "Good answer." This brief exchange has always stayed vivid in my mind because it demonstrates the first reality anyone must learn about western water issues:

Western water issues are about politics, not policy.

Most government agencies operate in a policy arena. Problems are investigated, alternative solutions considered, budgets proposed and debated, and problems addressed through policies developed in a cooperative fashion. The overriding objective is to identify and solve problems for the benefit of the taxpayers or an important constituency.

That isn't the case in the water world. No problem, budget, or solution is addressed in an unbiased and detached manner. Politics permeate every decision, every issue, and every attempted solution.

Senator Domenici clearly understood that his question had two dimensions. On the one hand, it was a policy question. Could the functions performed by a federal agency be performed by another entity? Clearly the answer was "yes." However, he had also asked a political question. Did he want to take the heat associated with abolishing an agency near and dear to the hearts of some of his constituents? Clearly, the answer was "no." Politics trump policy.

I once asked another Bureau commissioner, who had been a state official, how he found his first few months in office. His response was immediate and emotional: "It's so political. Everything I do is wrapped up in politics. It wasn't this way in state government."

———

Shortly after the Senate confirmed me as the new commissioner of the Bureau of Reclamation, I cleaned out my office on Capitol Hill and moved into my new office a few blocks away from the Lincoln Memorial. I was still unpacking boxes when I received a call from an old friend who worked as a lobbyist.

"I have a new client!" he began.

"Terrific," I said. "Who do you have to lobby?"

"You."

Since my agency oversaw the construction of water projects, I expected to hear from a lot of lobbyists. I agreed to my friend's request to meet for lunch. I asked, just before hanging up, "By the way, what's this about?"

"My client," he explained, "is a small town that is going to have its power rates quadrupled to pay for a hundred million dollar visitor's center you've built at Hoover Dam."

"One hundred million dollars?" I shouted. In the early 1990s, the Bureau had overseen the construction of a 20,000 square-foot visitor's center building with a parking lot, observation deck, and exhibit areas overlooking Hoover Dam. The original cost estimate was an extravagant $32 million. The idea that it could have cost $100 million was absurd. That's more than it cost to construct the dam itself or the Holocaust Museum near the Mall in Washington, D.C. "There's no way we could have spent that much on one building," I insisted.

He assured me that we had.

As soon as I hung up I called in my deputy, a thirty-year veteran of the agency, and told him a lobbyist claimed we had spent $100 million on a visitor's center.

"Impossible," he snapped, "I know we had problems with the

construction, but it couldn't have been that expensive." He promised to check into it.

Days later he returned saying that he had good news and bad news.

"The good news is," he said, "the visitor's center isn't going to cost $100 million."

"Well, give me the bad news," I said.

"Our team managing the project predicts it will cost $108 million, and there is a good chance costs could go up even higher."

At that moment—with my deputy in front of me looking at his shoe tops and shifting his weight from one foot to the other— I thought about my options. There were no good ones, only bad ones, very bad ones, and really, really bad ones. I saw little choice but to blow the whistle on my own agency.

Working with my press assistant, we called all the television news producers at the networks to see if they were interested in broadcasting the story. Initially, no one bit. Then a new, young producer at CNN agreed to run the story.

The reaction was immediate. The other networks called and demanded to know why they hadn't been alerted. Not to be outdone by CNN, they sent crews to the visitor's center near Las Vegas and put together their versions. I was a willing participant in every story, offering my outrage about what had happened and vowing to take action to ensure that we never built another "Taj Mahal in the Desert."

I recount this story about the Hoover Dam Visitor's Center because it brings up a second oddity about western water issues:

Logic and common sense seldom play a role in resolving water problems.

For some reason, when it comes to water-related issues, we toss common sense aside and usually pick the most illogical way to address problems. In this case, there was a need for a new visitor's center at Hoover Dam. Close to a million people visit the facility each year and the old center was inadequate to safely handle these visitors. But rather than focus on the best way to provide visitor services in a safe and efficient manner, common sense was cast aside in favor of building a monument at Hoover Dam.

The western landscape is filled with illogical projects that defy common sense. The Bureau of Reclamation, with congressional support, built an outrageously expensive desalting plant in Yuma, Arizona, when we could have solved the problem by retiring a few acres of irrigated farmland. To add insult to injury, the plant has operated just eight months in the last thirty years because it wasn't needed. When state officials handed out too many permits to pump ground water, we built dams and canals at federal expense to correct their mistakes when the simplest solution was to deny the pumping permits. We make water available at rock-bottom prices and then wonder why people won't conserve. And the list of illogical decisions goes on and on.

A few weeks after the Hoover Dam Visitor's Center media frenzy, Senator Mark Hatfield of Oregon, the chairman of the Senate Appropriations Committee, asked to meet with me. He had a reputation as being passionate about history and for taking moderate, middle-of-the-road positions. I felt lucky that my first meeting on Capitol Hill about the visitor's center would be with Senator Hatfield. I was sure it would be a reasoned discussion centered on the facts, and he would have suggestions for the best way to deal with the issue.

Leading up to the meeting, I spent a week gathering data, preparing reports, and holding briefings with my staff. I was armed with facts and intelligent recommendations for handling the present crisis and preventing it from happening again.

After the usual opening banter, Senator Hatfield got down to business. "Commissioner," he said, "what I'm concerned about is President Herbert Hoover. I strongly believe President Hoover is one of our most maligned Presidents and historians have done him a disservice."

What?

He continued: "I gave the Bureau of Reclamation a bust of President Hoover to display at the Hoover Dam Visitor's Center. It has come to my attention that the bust is not currently in the plans for the center, and I want this oversight corrected."

Speechless, I moved back in my chair and took several deep breaths. We had just discovered, and announced to the world, that we were going to spend $108 million or more on one building, exceeding our cost estimate by 430 percent. The cost to construct this edifice was over $5000 per square foot. We could have funded nutrition programs for poor children, financed cancer research, or done hundreds of other worthwhile things with that money.

Yet the senator with the responsibility for overseeing federal spending was concerned only that a bust he had given to our agency was not going to be prominently displayed at the center. Obviously I was missing something. Wasn't he concerned about our cost controls? Review procedures? Congressional notifications?

I promised the senator that President Hoover would be prominently displayed at the visitor's center. "We will not malign President Hoover," I told him. As a Democrat, I remember thinking that it would be a good idea to associate a Republican with this Taj Mahal of a visitor's center.

He smiled and thanked me. Our meeting was over.

This brings us to a third anomaly about western water issues: *Politicians don't care how much we spend to address water problems.*

Senator Hatfield didn't even mention the cost of the visitor's center the day we met. And why should he? Most members of Congress, as well as those who benefit from projects, never seem to be concerned about how much we're spending and why. They just assume that whatever amount of money they need will always be available.

As a public official, I felt an obligation to solve problems in the most inexpensive manner possible. The first time I appeared before the House Appropriations Committee as commissioner I felt a sense of pride that we were requesting less money than the Congress had provided the previous year. Imagine my surprise when committee members chided me for not requesting more. To them, an expanding budget was a badge of honor. This wouldn't be the last time I learned that my desire to solve water problems in the least expensive manner would be out of step with our political leaders.

When I think about the never-ending desire to spend money on water issues, I'm reminded of Edward Bennett Williams, the former owner of the Washington Redskins. Shortly after firing George Allen as his coach, he commented on Allen's insatiable desire to spend money to acquire new players: "I gave him an unlimited budget and he exceeded it."

———————

In May 2006, Fresno, California, Mayor Alan Autry held a press conference to announce his support for the construction of a new dam and reservoir on the San Joaquin River to provide flood control during wet years and water supply during dry years. It had been more than six decades, he observed, since a dam had been built in the area, and it was apparent to the mayor that a dam was needed now.

There were just a few problems with the mayor's promotion of the Temperance Flat Dam project. No one was sure a new dam would provide the needed flood protection or the water supply in dry years. Even the dam promoters didn't know if there was a suitable location. No one knew how much it would cost, they didn't know who would pay for it, they didn't know who would benefit from it, and they didn't know the environmental impacts associated with the dam. Despite these questions, Fresno city leaders were promoting a dam project costing somewhere between $2.5 billion and $3.5 billion.

Mayor Autry was elected after a successful career in the film and television industry. I'm sure he would never have embarked on a film project without first doing significant market research, creating a budget for the project, knowing where he was going to shoot the film, and how he was going to market the final product. Yet he promoted construction of a dam and reservoir at an undetermined location, of unknown size, indefinite cost, and unspecified benefit. Why do water projects cause prudent, thoughtful people to lose their common sense?

This willingness to promote a solution even before the most basic information is known is not that uncommon and it provides us with another reality about water issues:

When it comes to water, people choose a solution and then search for a problem to solve.

When it comes to water, we seem to go about things backward. We settle on a solution first and then we work backward, defining the problem based on the solution we've chosen. Temperance Flat Dam was a solution and it was chosen before anyone knew what the problem was.

Why we take this leapfrog approach has always been a mystery to me. It is important to understand that this curious way of thinking is not confined to one political party or one ideology.

In July 2012, Governor Jerry Brown of California and Interior Secretary Ken Salazar stepped in front of a bank of microphones and cameras to announce the Bay Delta Conservation Plan, which was designed to address the water problems associated with the Sacramento–San Joaquin River delta and estuary. This ambitious and comprehensive federal-state proposal was heralded as the solution to California's present and future water problems. The plan, they assured us, delicately balanced the competing demands of all Californians. Southern California cities and agribusiness would get additional water. Environmentalists would get a host of new programs and protections. Delta water quality would be protected and fisheries enhanced.

The solution according to Governor Brown was to construct twin 35-mile long pipelines, each about the size of a three-lane highway, that would tap river water and convey it under the Sacramento–San Joaquin River delta for conveyance south to farms and cities. This system would replace the present system of pumping water through the delta.

Governor Brown and Secretary Salazar were full of superlatives and assurances, but short on details in their announcement. "This proposal," Governor Brown said, "balances the concerns of those who live and work in the delta, those who rely on it for water, and those who appreciate its beauty, fish, waterfowl, and wildlife." Secretary Salazar said they had forged a "lasting and sustainable solution that strengthens California's water security and restores the health of the delta [using] science as our guide."

Once again, the politicians got the cart before the horse. How much would it cost? The first estimates were just short of $15 billion. Who would pay for it? They weren't exactly sure, although they claimed they were committed to a "user pay" principle, but details were vague. How much water would go through the pipeline, and what time of year would it be available? They didn't say. Where would this water come from? They were silent on that point. What were the benefits and costs of the project? Once again, silence. Finally, how long would it take to construct the project? The estimate was a decade *after* all the environmental and engineering studies and permits had been completed. No one knew when that would be.

Once the euphoria of the announcement faded, things got worse for project proponents. The costs skyrocketed to at least $25 billion and probably more. Northern California newspapers skewered the plan and ratepayers balked at paying additional costs. The lack of project details inflamed the debate and cheaper alternatives began to emerge.

As a congressional staff person, there were numerous times when I was visited by advocates who would say, "We're here to urge your boss's support of our dam." Then I would ask, "Why do you want to build a dam? What is the problem you're trying to solve?" Nine times out of ten, the answer I got was silence.

Trying to make sense of the decisions we've made on water issues is a real challenge for the average person. When I first started working on these issues, I felt like I had fallen down the rabbit hole with Alice into Wonderland. Things just didn't make any sense. But slowly, as I moved from issue to issue, things got clearer if I remembered that water is a world rife with politics and devoid of common sense, fiscal responsibility, and logical decision-making.

But my experiences began in the 1970s. Surely, we've improved things over the past forty years. I'm afraid not.

Every year, members of the Sacramento Metropolitan Chamber of Commerce journey to Washington, D.C., for their "Cap-to-Cap," or Capitol-to-Capitol, lobbying trip. Chamber leaders come to rattle their tin cups, looking for federal dollars for an assortment of federally funded projects.

In 2006, they provided the new chairman of the House Appropriations Committee, California Congressman Jerry Lewis, an opportunity to speak at one of their luncheons. His remarks that day were somewhat unusual. Rather than mention all the projects of interest to chamber leaders, Mr. Lewis turned the tables and used the lunch as an opportunity to lobby the chamber. He proclaimed that the era of big dams was not over, and he urged the organization to support the construction of Auburn Dam on the American River upstream of Sacramento. If they would endorse a multipurpose Auburn Dam, "I am sure we would be responsive," he told the chamber officials.

Lewis's statements were not prompted by research or investigations concluding that there was a critical need for the dam. His call was based on re-election politics. Congressman John Doolittle, a member of Lewis's committee, had championed the construction of Auburn Dam throughout his career. With a series of ethics and fundraising scandals putting his re-election in doubt, Doolittle had resurrected the dam project as part of his election-year strategy. Lewis was supporting the dam to help his colleague get re-elected.

Auburn Dam is one of the worst projects ever conceived by Bureau of Reclamation planners. It is an outrageously expensive, dangerous, and useless project. The project was conceived as a thin-arch, concave concrete dam to impound the American River to provide irrigation and municipal water supplies, power, and flood control. I mention the original design, which looked something like a bowl on its side, because that was the primary reason the planners wanted to build the dam. It was going to be a technological first for concrete dams, and the engineers couldn't wait to get started. Since it was being built in the district of a powerful congressional com-mittee chairman, former Congressman Bizz Johnson, the Bureau was assured of long-term congressional support.

In 1977, during excavation for the base of the dam, an earth-quake fault line was discovered running through the base of the proposed dam site. Not *near* the dam site but *through* it. Work stopped, and the scientists began to scratch their heads and con-sult. Was this an active fault? What was the probability of a future quake? Could a safe dam be built at the site? After years of analysis, it was concluded that a safe dam could be built, but it would have to be a large, earthen dam looking something like a giant beanbag.

The engineers were not interested in building a "beanbag" dam, and Congressman Johnson had retired. The project was dead. For nearly forty years the excavation site for the dam sat abandoned, except for a lonely watchman. Dam promoters clung to the hope that some day they would be able to build a dam, and repeated efforts were made to resurrect it as a flood control project, but even that proposal couldn't get approved.

By 2008, Congressman Doolittle was hopelessly entangled in the Abramoff Affairs and was forced to retire. But hope springs eternal when it comes to dam projects. Mr. Doolittle was replaced by Congressman Tom McClintock, who took over the task of blowing on the embers of hope for Auburn Dam. He has certainly been up to the task. He rarely misses a chance to tote the dam's virtues. In 2014, for example, he pronounced "completion of that project would mean four-hundred-year flood protection for Sacramento and ... enough clean, cheap hydroelectricity to power a million homes and a major new recreational center in our region."

What he conveniently ignores, however, besides building a dam on a known fault line, is that over the past forty years, the costs of the project have soared into the financial stratosphere. Rather than costing $425 million as originally thought, the project would now cost well north of $3 to $4 billion. The water marketed from this dam, if it were built, would be the most expensive water ever developed in California. A recent benefit-cost analysis has not been prepared on the project, but if one is prepared, we'll find that the project will return mere pennies for every dollar we invest.

It seems that we still haven't learned anything new when it comes to water. A grossly expensive solution is being promoted even before we've decided what the problem is that we're trying to solve.

Logic, common sense, fiscal responsibility, and thoughtful decision-making have all taken a back seat to the politics of re-electing politicians.

2

The Water Nobility

We need to stop catering to the Water Nobility,
who have secured a grip on western water.

The United States built 70,000 dams between 1900 and 1970. That's an average of nearly three dams per day. In fact, 85 percent of the dams in America were constructed during that seventy-year span, known as the golden age of concrete.

During this period, we went on a dam- and canal-building binge unrivaled by any nation on the globe. The solution to every water problem seemed to be the same—pour concrete. If we were looking for one symbol to characterize twentieth-century America, a dam might be a good choice.

At the beginning of the last century, the federal government created the Bureau of Reclamation to build dams and water projects to promote settlement and economic development in the West. Many engineering marvels were constructed, but none was more important than Hoover Dam. Completed in 1936, it provided the launching pad for the Bureau's glory years. Now nearly eighty years old, Hoover Dam (originally called Boulder Dam) is still a magnificent engineering accomplishment. Construction was completed in just five years by a unique management team and workers who endured harsh working conditions. When it was completed, it was viewed as one of the wonders of the world, and it still is today.

But Hoover Dam represented something more important. It represented the beginning of the "Go-Go Years" in which scores of big dam projects (all trying to outdo Hoover Dam) were built.

This was a freewheeling, free-spending approach to the construction of water projects because they were viewed as critical for reducing unemployment, generating power, and "managing" natural resources. Economics didn't matter at all. As Marc Reisner, who chronicled this era in *Cadillac Desert* noted, if the projects "... slide into an ocean of debt, the huge hydroelectric dams authorized within the same river basin could generate the necessary revenues to bail them out (or so it was thought). It was a breathtakingly audacious solution to an intractable problem, and the results were to be breathtaking as well."

Millions of yards of concrete were poured, and dams rose across the West. It was thought to be a program at the vanguard of progress—irrigating the western deserts, creating jobs, inspiring a generation.

The government hired Woody Guthrie to write a song glorifying dams, and he toured the Pacific Northwest singing the wonders of dam construction:

You jus' watch this river 'n pretty soon
Everybody's gonna be changin' their tune ...
That big Grand Coulee 'n Bonneville Dam'll
Build a thousand factories f'r Uncle Sam

The Go-Go Years of building water projects no matter what the price was an inspiration to the next few generations of engineers and planners. They wanted to join the parade of projects. They believed whole-heartedly in the positive attributes of water projects. After all, they offered a solution to the Dust Bowl, created jobs, and enriched people's lives. They were the stuff of folklore and song. They were transforming the landscape of the West. They were bringing progress. These were noble efforts and exciting times, especially for the engineers at the Bureau of Reclamation. The group that would become the Water Nobility was an integral part of this entire effort. They were the recipients of the benefits, and they were the cheerleaders urging a willing Congress and successive Presidents to continue the effort.

In the early years, no one questioned the need for such water projects. The *modus operandi* for solving water problems was simple—pour concrete. Threatened by a flood? Build a dam. Need cheap water for agriculture? Build a dam and a canal. Need cheap power? Build a dam and a hydroelectric power plant.

Starting in the 1970s, however, we entered a new phase. The last of the big water projects had been authorized in Congress. The bureaucracy was busy completing construction and Congress was intent on bringing home the funds to make sure these projects were finished.

But for the first time, a President questioned the need for these projects and demanded stronger justification. In 1977, President Carter developed a "hit list" of water projects he did not want to build. This decision was a slap in the face to the projects' congressional sponsors, as well as local sponsors, shaking the "I scratch your back, you scratch mine" system to its very core.

But it had another effect. Whether consciously or unconsciously, the hit list caused the water development community to focus their efforts in a new direction. Instead of just working to build more dams, they also began to focus on gaining permanent control over the water and other benefits made available through the dam-building program. This meant they needed to develop a new set of talents and skills like those of a corporate raider.

Like a corporate raider, the water development community began quietly working to gain control of public assets and investments. They worked to make these assets *their* property. In a sense, they changed from being a "booster club" into a group of "owners" who believed they were entitled to permanently receive a federal benefit.

As they engaged in this process, they began to think of themselves as a noble class. They were no longer just the beneficiaries of a federal program at the behest of the federal taxpayers. They came to view the entire effort as their own personal real estate and investment portfolio. The projects built by the taxpayers became "their" projects; the financial payments and subsidies they received was "their" money. They developed their own curious sense of ownership of a federal program. They began to feel it was right that they should receive these projects and money because what they were doing was just and noble. Because it was their property and their money, it was logical in their minds that they should have permanent control of these assets.

The Water Nobility had arrived.

While commissioner, I accepted an invitation from local officials to visit Klamath Falls, Oregon, to speak at a public forum.

The Klamath River Basin straddles the Oregon-California border some one hundred miles from the coast. A federal dam my agency built and maintained impounds the water in Klamath Lake, and the water is released for irrigation in the basin.

But irrigation isn't the only use of the water. This area is also an important stop on the Pacific Flyway, where millions of birds congregate during the spring and fall migrations at six national wildlife refuges in the Klamath Basin. After the water meets these needs, it flows down the Klamath River into northern California, generating electricity and providing flows for migrating salmon that are important to the local Indian tribes and commercial salmon fishermen as the river makes its way to the Pacific Ocean. Delivering water to meet the needs of these sometimes competing interests was my agency's responsibility. This had historically been an easy job. The Klamath Basin was once described as a huge sponge that soaked up groundwater for thousands of years, and surface water flows were adequate to meet all the needs. Farmers who had been encouraged to settle the area after World War I, wildlife advocates, fishermen, and the tribes coexisted in an uneasy equilibrium in this spongy environment.

By the mid-1990s, however, this equilibrium was beginning to crumble. Six years of drought, plus no willingness on the part of anyone to decrease their use of water, resulted in the first shortages in over ninety years. Deliveries of water to farmers were reduced and they screamed loudly and berated their congressional delegation, demanding relief.

They weren't the only unhappy customers. Hunters and wildlife advocates, including the U.S. Fish and Wildlife Service, which operated the refuges, wanted more water for their needs. Commercial salmon fishermen and the Hoopa and Yurok Indians (who relied on migrating salmon) wanted more water released into the river to guarantee fish flows. Just to add some spice, several salmon species were teetering on the edge of being designated as endangered. They desperately needed additional flows in the river to enable them to migrate to and from spawning grounds.

It was a volatile mix of competing interests, and I had been asked to attend a "community meeting" to discuss the problem.

Like so many other times, I put in a full day in Washington, D.C. then took a late afternoon flight to Denver, where I changed planes to Portland. Arriving around 7:30 p.m. Portland time (10:30 Eastern time), I boarded a flight to Klamath Falls, arriving around 9:30 p.m. Taking three different flights and arriving for an after midnight (my time) meeting, I was a little rummy.

When we pulled into the community center, I noticed police cars and asked what they were for. "They're for you," I was told.

We proceeded into the hall, where a standing room-only crowd of agitated farmers, local business leaders, police, and media met me. It was a hot, steamy room, and the locals were out for my blood.

After trying to break the ice with some humorous remarks, I was interrupted by a very agitated lady. "How dare you people come here from Washington, D.C. and make fun of this situation," she snarled, with contempt dripping off every word. "It's people like you that are putting us out of business by refusing to deliver us water. It's our water. We paid for it, and we want you to deliver it—now!"

She turned out to be the most compassionate and understanding person who spoke that evening. Others simply shouted and berated me.

As the meeting attendees continued their assault, I came to two conclusions: First, I'd been set up. I looked over at the local person who had invited me, and he had a very big grin on his face as he watched his friends and neighbors pummel me.

Second, the people shouting at me truly didn't understand what was happening to them. They had been farming their land for ninety years without interruption. The federal government had encouraged them to settle the area, built them a water project and supplied them with low-cost water and power. Their livelihood was intimately interwoven with the water project and the benefits it supplied.

It had been a wonderful ninety years for nearly all these people. They made a good living nestled in a magnificent part of the country. Now people and issues that they didn't understand threatened their world. They didn't care about wildlife or salmon. They didn't care about the needs of commercial fishermen, Indian tribes, or refuge managers. This was "their" project, "their" water, and "their" livelihood.

The people shouting at me had become members of the Water Nobility.

What is the Water Nobility? It is an unofficial, loose-knit collection of people spread across the seventeen western states who receive water from federal dams and an associated cadre of politicians, lawyers, lobbyists, engineers, government officials, and others who work with them. Once they were grateful recipients of a federal program, but at some point in time, they began to view the benefits as an entitlement, even a birthright. They came to believe that they should receive federal funds and resources in perpetuity. To them, this wasn't welfare or subsidies. They were investments—a wise use of taxpayer dollars, and it was theirs.

In the view of the Water Nobility, by providing them with

water and subsidies at federal expense and allowing them to benefit is good for America. Abstractions like "fairness," "equality," or "majority rule" are irrelevant. The only issue is the continued flow of money and power.

The Water Nobility has evolved all across the West over the past forty years. It isn't limited to farmers. Those cities, towns, and other organizations that benefit from water projects have become accustomed to the benefits they receive, and they are assuming ownership. They are joined by local business leaders, lawyers, lobbyists, and others who benefit from the system. In some cases, this change is taking place consciously; in other places, it is happening unconsciously.

The Water Nobility has become a pervasive force largely because of the generous assistance and recognition it has received from the Congress. This is ironic given an interesting provision in the Constitution. The framers of the Constitution had a strong dislike for the British nobility and were determined to make sure a rigid class system didn't develop in the United States. As a result, they inserted Article I, Section 9, which outlines a series of specific actions that Congress may not take, and among them is the admonition that "No title of nobility shall be granted by the United States ..." The founding fathers wanted to make sure we didn't establish a peerage composed of barons and baronesses, viscounts, earls, and other nobility.

But through its actions over the past forty years, Congress has created a *de facto* "title of nobility" for those who receive water from western water projects. As we shall see in the following pages, we have given a small group of people an exalted status, and we've paid to underwrite their lifestyle and put hundreds of millions of dollars in their pockets for reasons that are hard to fathom. It is time we recognize what we've been doing and put a stop to it. The general public is unaware of the Water Nobility, and national leaders have been unwilling to stand up to them. The Nobility has buffaloed the public, the press, and politicians into thinking that it is logical and right that they should receive more federal funds and secure permanent control over a significant portion of water in the West.

A key component of the Water Nobility's success has been their ability to develop and perpetuate a number of myths about western water.

Myth Number 1: There is a direct relationship between the growth in population and a need for more water.

Today, the West accounts for one-third of the nation's total population, and it is the fastest growing region of the country. In 2013, seven of the ten largest cities in America were located west of the Mississippi River, and this growth in population has occurred in a unique manner. The West has developed into a series of "urban archipelagos" consisting of cities and suburbs with great population densities surrounded by open space and rural areas. While about 75 percent of people in the East live in metropolitan areas, 86 percent of westerners reside in or near cities.

And there doesn't seem to be any let-up in this growth. As of 2010, four of the six largest counties in America are in the West. The growth in Maricopa County, Arizona, is nothing short of staggering—between 2000 and 2005 it grew by 563,000 people. Even the Great Recession couldn't impact the increase. From 2010 to 2013, the county grew by nearly 200,000 residents, a 5 percent growth rate.

Conventional wisdom would suggest that, with so many more people moving to western urban centers, there is greater need to build more water projects to supply more water.

Conventional wisdom is wrong.

There is no direct correlation between the growth in population and a need for more water. While we will have to build more delivery lines to supply people with water in growing western cities, it doesn't necessarily follow that we will have to build more reservoirs, dams, and other facilities.

Let's take California as an example. Between 1975 and 2001, the state's population grew by 60 percent, and the gross state product grew two and one-half times. That is significant growth by any standard. Los Angeles uses less water—about 129 gallons per person per day—than almost any other big American city. More importantly, that figure is down from 172 gallons in 1980. Today, Los Angeles' 2.9 million residents use less water than they did forty years ago when it had one million fewer residents.

As water expert Peter Gleick has noted, in the past thirty years we have "broken the link between the growth of our population and economy and the size of our water demands." Water conservation programs have helped, but so have improvements in technology and water use. In the 1960s, we produced only $1 in goods and services for every hundred gallons of water we used. Today, we produce more than $10 for every hundred gallons used, even correcting for inflation.

Myth Number 2: We need to provide subsidized water to agriculture to meet the food and fiber needs of our nation.

Every time the Water Nobility testifies before Congress, they have one mantra they use over and over. "Subsidized irrigation is critical if this nation is to meet the food and fiber needs of a growing population."

Hogwash! The number of acres in irrigated agriculture in the West (and throughout the country) has declined steadily over the past twenty-five years. The U.S. Census Bureau reported that irrigated acreage has fallen by 25 percent since 1988. Yet, since the 1980s, production from irrigated agriculture has continued to increase, and the monetary value of crops grown has also increased.

As a business and way of life, irrigated agriculture is changing. Western irrigated farms that are smaller than ten acres or larger than five hundred acres have increased, while midsize farms have decreased. Obviously, two things are happening at once. Small, hobby farms are increasing, and through consolidation, the larger operations are getting larger at the expense of more modest size farms.

The argument that we need to subsidize irrigated agriculture to meet national food and fiber needs is false.

Myth Number 3: The majority of water in western communities is consumed by swimming pools, golf courses, fountains, and other amenities.

I wish Steve Wynn had never built the water fountain that catches on fire at the Mirage Hotel in Las Vegas. Everyone seems to have seen the fountain. Every night it puts on a spectacular show every hour from 7:00 p.m. until midnight. It shoots thousands of gallons of water into the air and at regular intervals, flames shoot up, bringing "oohs" and "ahs" from the hundreds of spectators. When I tell people I work on western water issues, they immediately say, "Oh yeah, that's really a problem. Have you ever seen that fountain in Las Vegas that catches on fire? Now that's a waste of water!"

It really isn't a waste since the water is reused for each show, and it's "gray water," meaning it is not fit to drink. But people don't like to know those pesky little details.

Here's what's important about western water use. Irrigated agriculture accounts for 85 percent of all the water consumed in the West depending on the location. All those rapidly growing urban archipelagos, with their swimming pools, lawns, golf courses, and fountains, and all the businesses and industries they've created, account for only 10 percent of all water consumed in the West.

So what is the water consumed by agriculture used for? Nearly two-thirds of it is used to produce low-value, high water-use forage for cattle.

Let's use California again as an example. Alfalfa irrigation is the single largest use of water in California. Harvested mostly for hay, alfalfa uses nearly 20 percent of the state's water and one-quarter of the state's irrigation water. By using all this water, alfalfa growers market a crop that accounts for only 4 percent of the state's agricultural revenue. To add insult to injury, alfalfa in California primarily uses flood-irrigation techniques. This approach is highly inefficient, resulting in only half the water actually getting to the crop. What is this alfalfa used for? More than 70 percent feeds dairy cattle that produce as much waste as a city of 21 million people. Much of the remaining alfalfa is exported to Japan.

Myth Number 4: The legal and policy issues surrounding water are best left to the experts because western water issues are complicated; the general public has no business being involved in solutions.

An important plank of the Nobility's platform is for the general public to be completely ignorant about what is going on. They don't want an informed public involved with their issues. They don't want anyone to know what is happening because they believe it isn't the public's business. Remember, these are "their" projects and "their" water. To avoid public disclosure and debate, a façade has been erected. "These are complicated issues," they say. "We're the experts; you should leave any solutions to us and our friends in Congress or the government agencies."

Western water isn't complicated. Obamacare is complicated. Your phone bill is complicated. Figuring out how the price of gas at your local gas station is established is complicated. Western water is not.

The group most responsible for trying to obfuscate the public is water lawyers. They love to confuse you with gobbledygook, mumbo-jumbo, and nonsense. They love to perpetuate the idea that water law is very complex and arcane. "Since it is such a difficult subject," they say, "you better leave the details to us."

Here's what you need to know about western water law. The laws were established for and have been implemented to meet the needs of irrigated agriculture and the mining industry. The laws are based on the premise that whoever used the water first can continue to use it as long as they don't waste it. This doctrine is called "first in time, first in right."

Water in all the western states was assumed to be free and was made available without regard to price. Western water was also "nationalized" and put under the control of the state governments. It then was allocated to potential users by state bureaucracies or boards based on the first in time, first in right doctrine.

There were a couple of exceptions to this rule. First, Indian tribes that had been using the water for centuries didn't count. Settlers and miners were allowed to take water from Indians with impunity. The second exception was "wasted" water. State boards determine waste and they rarely, if ever, determined that a farmer or miner was wasting water.

If you think this policy sounds somewhat like the old Soviet communist economic system, you're right. Price and markets have nothing to do with the distribution of resources. If you get there first, begin to use the water and convince people in the government to give it to you, you can keep it. It is a rigid system that uses government command and control and history as the allocation mechanisms.

How effective is this system? That depends on who you ask. It's a great system for water lawyers, farmers, and mining companies. It's a terrible system for environmentalists who want water in the river, Indian tribes who want their water returned, or cities settled after the initial distribution of the water rights.

There's something else wrong with this system. It is not kind to western rivers and streams. The vast majority of these rivers and streams are over-allocated, meaning that the state water boards have given away more water than what was in the river or stream. Why? Because it was difficult to look their neighbors in the eye and say "no" when they asked for more water. And the water boards had an ace up their sleeve. To rectify their mistakes, they, accompanied by the Water Nobility, came to Washington, D.C. looking

for the taxpayers to provide money to build a water storage project
to compensate for their inability to say "no."

Western water laws have erected a terribly archaic and inefficient distribution system that doesn't meet the needs of a modern
West with millions of people living in urban archipelagos. Urban
residents want water in a stream for fishing, hunting, river raft-
ing, kayaking, or just plain enjoyment. The present legal system
was designed to do just the opposite; it allows farmers to dry up
a stream so they can grow one more cutting of hay in August or
September.

3

Picking Your Pocket for Billions

*The federal government should not subsidize
the delivery of water from its projects.*

Over 85 percent of all the water consumed in the West is used by agriculture. That's right, 85 percent. Nearly all this water is used to irrigate crops and the federal government supplies one-half of it.

What is water supplied by the federal government used for? A majority of it is used to produce alfalfa, hay, and other grasses for the cattle industry. The farms that consume this water don't pay fair market value prices for it. Instead, they receive the water at highly reduced rates through a complex set of subsidy payments from federal taxpayers.

Because of subsidies, marginal farms continue to operate and uneconomic water uses and farming practices are perpetuated. Water that may be desperately needed for high priority environmental or urban uses continues to flow to farms because of the western water subsidy system.

These subsidies are a raid on our pocketbooks. They deprive the treasury of billions of dollars in revenue that must be made up by taxpayers or by increasing the national debt. We've deregulated the airline industry, the telephone industry, and a host of other industries in this country and throughout the world. Congress has even toyed with the idea of eliminating crop subsidies for agriculture. How much longer can we avoid facing the issue of providing water from western water projects at highly subsidized rates? We provide our most valuable resource to this select group of users at rates that are impossible to justify. We give this select group of users an outdated and unjustified subsidy that gives them an artificial competitive advantage that lasts a lifetime. Even worse, our largesse promotes excessive use and drives water away from other high priority uses.

Challenge anyone to give an answer to this simple statement: The federal taxpayers should continue to provide hundreds of millions of dollars each year in subsidies to agricultural users of water from western water projects because _____. No one could develop an answer that would withstand taxpayer scrutiny in every section of the country.

———

Understanding the benefits that the Water Nobility receives requires an understanding of how subsidies are provided by Congress.

The foundation for the entire system is the use of zero interest loans, with unbelievably attractive repayment terms combined with other benefits. Assume you've just bought a $200,000 home, with no down payment, in a suburban real estate development called "Subsidy Acres." Compare paying for the house using normal mortgage terms versus the repayment terms required for western water projects.

Assuming you could get a forty-year, fixed-rate mortgage for the entire $200,000 at 4.25 percent interest, you would pay a total of $416,275 for the home ($200,000 plus interest of $216,275). But if you bought the same house with a forty-year, zero interest loan, it would only cost a total of $200,000.

Of course, you don't need to start repaying this loan right away. Congress graciously provided water project recipients with a ten-year grace period *before* they had to start making their subsidized payments.

But wait, there's more. The Water Nobility only has to pay that portion of the loan they're able to pay based on their anticipated income over the next forty years. And who makes this "ability to pay" calculation? Their friends in the Bureau of Reclamation. This is almost a laughable calculation for the Bureau personnel since no one can accurately predict your income and expenses for the next forty years, and your ability to repay any loan no matter how small.

The most a farmer in our example would likely pay (based on actual examples) would be about $80,000. With a conventional mortgage, your monthly payment would have been $984 for forty years and you would have paid $416,275 for the house. But if you get a subsidized loan, you would pay only $166 a month for forty years—a total of $80,000 for the house, but only after you had waited ten years before starting to repay the loan.

The largesse doesn't stop there—the federal government isn't done handing out subsidies. Since Subsidy Acres is a multi-decade real estate development, you won't have to begin making payments until the entire project is "substantially complete." This could be decades down the road. In addition, you will get electric power provided at rates that would make a Scotsman blush—in some cases at discounts of 50 to 75 percent of market price.

And even better, if you can't make any of these payments for any reason, the federal government will let you defer payments without interest or penalty for as long as you like.

This is how western water projects are "repaid." A recent General Accountability Office report found that irrigators paid only 21 percent of the $6.4 billion in construction costs assigned to them, and the remainder was either written off or paid by power users.

The story of how this generous set of repayment subsidies developed begins with a charismatic character named John Wesley Powell. Major Powell was a one-armed Civil War veteran who gained fame as the first white man to float down the Colorado River through the Grand Canyon in 1869. Powell retraced this journey in 1871 and 1872.

Although his expeditions were a disaster in many respects, his promotional abilities were second to none. After returning from his expeditions, he hit the lecture circuit and wrote a best-selling journal of his expedition. His exploits captivated an American public yearning for adventure in the West, and Powell became rich and famous.

Powell was equally adept as a lobbyist and promoter of government programs. He was instrumental in the establishment of the U.S. Geological Survey and was the Survey's second director from 1881–1894. In an unusual case of double-dipping, he also served at the same time as the director of the Smithsonian Institution's Bureau of Ethnology. But it was his ability to encourage Congress to promote settlement of the West and pass laws to assist this development that was his lasting accomplishment.

One such law was the Reclamation Act of 1902, passed after much debate in Congress. This law laid out how the federal government would help build dams to assist settlement in the arid West. The Reclamation Act established a ten-year loan program to finance projects. It also mandated that only farms of 160 acres or less could receive the loans and the loan recipient had to live on the land—no corporate farms or absentee landlords in this program.

The program was a financial disaster. Loan defaults began almost immediately, and Congress quickly lengthened the repayment period by another ten years. To help out, the Interior Department regulators conveniently forgot about enforcing the residency requirement for loan recipients.

Even these changes didn't work. Within twenty years, 60 percent of those receiving water from Bureau projects were defaulting on their payments, and by 1927, over one-third of Reclamation farmers had sold their lands to speculators.

Then the Congress got really creative. It set up a repayment system that was a marvel of ingenuity and special interest favors. Legislators doubled the loan repayment period again—to forty or more years—and directed that Bureau project recipients receive zero interest loans and electric power generated at federal dams at greatly reduced rates. The Interior Department joined the "reform" effort by inventing the "ability to pay" concept described earlier.

At this point, the supporters of federal irrigated agriculture got lucky. The Great Depression provided an entirely new justification for federal involvement in dam building. Instead of being an agricultural program, the entire effort became a jobs program. Dams and canals were justified by how many jobs they could provide to a job-hungry nation. World War II continued the good luck. With the nation focused on the war effort, the construction of dams to assist agriculture faded as jobs and electricity for factories took on importance.

The nation then went on the dam-building binge mentioned earlier. Large projects such as the Hoover, Shasta, and Grand Coulee Dams became permanent fixtures on the landscape. The western United States was literally transformed by these projects. Our West became an area where water projects enabled us to build and sustain large communities in areas that are natural deserts. By 2013, for example, seven of the ten largest counties in America were located in the West and four of the seven depended on western water projects for an important part of their water supply.

Why should the taxpayers care about this? The short answer is because it's your money—you pay for it. The term "subsidy" means someone gets a good or service from the government at a reduced rate. In this case, the taxpayers provided a water project to a select group of farmers and western business interests. An agreement was reached for reasonable repayment of the money used to construct the projects. But through laughable accounting and legal maneuvers, Congress has allowed the Water Nobility to make a mockery of the repayment system. They've cooked the books. Rather than require the recipients to pay for the project, they got you to pay for it.

How much are you paying? The Congressional Budget Office last calculated the total program subsidy in the late 1980s. If we update their figures for inflation, the total subsidy for the Bureau of Reclamation program would be an astounding $56 to $116 billion!

Congressman George Miller (D-CA) once remarked that western water interests received so much in subsidies that they could "grow aluminum" in their fields. Based on the Congressional Budget Office estimates, he wasn't far off.

In 2013, the western water system delivered water to 140,000 operations farming ten million acres of land. The subsidy works out to be somewhere between $5,600 and $12,000 per acre, which is more than most of the land is worth.

The subsidy doesn't stop there. Remember the requirement that the first payment doesn't start until the project is "substantially complete"? Consider construction on the Central Valley Project in California. It began delivering irrigation water in 1940, but the Interior Department never certified the project as substantially complete. Those receiving water from the project didn't start to repay capital costs of the project until Congress passed legislation in 1986. This legislation requires the water users to complete repayment of the project by 2030—ninety years after water was first delivered from the project.

Unfortunately, it gets worse. The most illogical of all subsidies is something called the "double subsidy." The best estimate we have is that nearly 45 percent of the farmers who receive irrigation water subsidies are growing crops that also receive price supports from the U.S. Department of Agriculture (USDA).

What does that mean in English? It means that these farms are growing crops the USDA believes there are already too much of and doesn't want them to be grown. The USDA pays farmers not to grow these "surplus" crops or it sets an artificial minimum price for the crop to protect farm incomes. If the market price goes below this target, the federal government buys these crops at the minimum price. Remember, the Bureau of Reclamation is providing subsidized water to encourage farmers to grow these crops. One politician correctly compared the double subsidy to driving with one foot on the gas and the other on the brake.

To make matters worse, many of the farmers using subsidized

water are growing crops of such low value that the subsidies they receive are worth more than the crop itself.

Who gets this double subsidy? The Bureau of Reclamation has avoided identifying the farms, but the Environmental Working Group, a nonprofit research and advocacy organization based in Washington, D.C., did a very interesting analysis of 6,800 farming operations in California's Central Valley. Using computer data from the USDA, Interior Department, and the state of California, they calculated the water and crop payments to each farm receiving federal water in 2002. Their conclusion was that these farms took in a total of $538 million in water and crop subsidies in that single year: the water subsidy was $416 million and the crop subsidy was $122 million.

The Interior Department's Inspector General has urged the practice be "discontinued expeditiously." The Government Accountability Office has repeatedly urged passage of legislation to eliminate this double subsidy, but Congress has refused to budge. For over forty years, Congress has considered scores of bills to eliminate double subsidy payments. None have made it to the President's desk for signature.

This system of subsidies was developed, and has lasted for more than a hundred years, through the combined efforts of the Water Nobility, their lobbyists, lawyers, and congressional supporters. It has been a truly bi-partisan effort.

It didn't matter whether western politicians were liberal or conservative, Democrat or Republican. They voted for water development, they supported retaining the subsidies, and they didn't question why. Former Senator Barry Goldwater, who was no friend of welfare, corporate or individual, was a lifelong supporter of western water projects in general and the Central Arizona Project in particular. Marc Reisner observed that the liberal former California governor, Jerry Brown, attended the funeral of E.F. Schumacher, the English economist who wrote *Small is Beautiful*, then flew back home to lobby for a water project that would cost more than it did to put a man on the moon.

This bi-partisan wall of support shouldn't surprise anyone. If there is one axiom about western politicians and water projects, it is this: Never stand between a western politician and a federal water project. No matter what they tell you when they run for office, once elected they undergo a water lobotomy, and as long as they're in office, they don't question the subsidies made available to western water projects. Once they leave office, their brain returns to functioning normally. It is the rare western politician who gathers up enough political courage to say "no" to the western water system.

———

Explaining the scandalous truth about western water to a non-believer isn't easy. During the Carter Administration, I worked at the Interior Department and was sent to Capitol Hill to brief former Congressman Berkeley Bedell on the program.

Since he was an Iowa congressman and familiar with farm programs, I assumed the briefing would last no more than twenty minutes. I was wrong.

I began to explain the financing of western water projects by saying that irrigation costs were calculated at the time of construction and repaid at zero percent interest over a forty-year period. Any costs beyond an irrigator's ability to pay would be repaid by power consumers starting forty years after the project was declared complete at zero percent interest.

"You what?" Bedell interrupted.

I repeated myself, only slower; he cut me off again.

"If I understand you correctly," he said, "this is supposed to be a loan program. But if what you say is correct, millions of dollars are going to be repaid at zero percent interest over nearly forty years, and millions more will be repaid in fifty or a hundred years at zero percent interest. That amounts to an unconscionable subsidy. Are you sure your explanation is right?"

He had honed in on the best-kept secret of western water: those who benefit from the program are reaping a financial windfall worth billions of dollars. More importantly, this is a benefit that comes year after year after year because it is a subsidy that has been firmly cemented into law and which is protected by local chambers of commerce, state officials, a federal cabinet department and members of Congress from both parties. One thing is clear. If members of Congress from states like Iowa aren't aware of this scam, the American taxpayer certainly is in the dark.

My scheduled twenty-minute briefing with the congressman ended up lasting nearly two hours. He grilled me on the program particulars and kept saying over and over, "Are you sure? This can't be right." When I assured him I was right, he kept saying with a certain amount of disbelief in his voice, "This is wrong, isn't it?"

I have to admit I dodged answering his question. As an administration official, my job was to support the President's program. The President was not interested in another fight with Congress over western water projects.

Nearly forty years later, I now have an answer for Congressman Bedell. Is this wrong? Yes, Congressman, it is wrong, and these subsidies should be eliminated. Enough is enough.

4
Bowling for Dollars

*The Bureau of Reclamation should be abolished
because it is an outdated bureaucracy.*

"I wouldn't hire the Bureau of Reclamation to build a doghouse!" Congressman George Miller thundered. "Every one of their projects has massive cost over-runs, every one is a huge environmental insult, every one is basically publicly unacceptable."

I had just gone to work for George as the staff director of the House of Representatives subcommittee that oversaw the Bureau of Reclamation and other western water issues. The subcommittee was always viewed as a pork-barrel committee, or as one newspaper account noted, it was the authorizing "spigot" for every major Bureau project from the Mississippi to the Pacific.

George had taken over as subcommittee chair and he was responding to a reporter's question about his agenda. George had a reputation for outspoken views on a wide variety of issues, and this reputation was bolstered by his six-foot-four-inch frame and his habit of loud, in-your-face, rough-and-tumble questioning of witnesses at congressional hearings.

His outburst was living up to this reputation, and it laid the foundation for an interesting run as subcommittee chair.

It was a slow Friday afternoon until I heard my coworker say from the other room, "You're not going to believe what the Bureau has done now."

"Try me," I said.

"They've built a bowling alley."

Even I wasn't prepared for that one.

The Central Utah Project (CUP) is a massive effort that makes you wonder who has the creativity and audacity to think up such an idea. The project consists of dozens of small dams and retention facilities that impound water in high mountain streams in eastern Utah. The water is then transported hundreds of miles in a series of canals and tunnels through the Wasatch Mountains to Salt Lake City and other cities and towns along the Wasatch Front.

The CUP was conceived in the 1930s and had been a dream of Utah politicians and business leaders for decades. Construction began in the 1960s and still continues today. The project has been reduced in size, primarily due to costs, but the basic dream continues: divert water flowing into the Colorado River, transport it across the state, and use it to meet the growing needs of Salt Lake City, Provo, and other Utah communities.

Duchesne, Utah, is a small, dusty town with few paved streets, four taverns, and four churches out among the sagebrush and juniper of eastern Utah. It is remote, but it has the distinction of being the only community in America with a $450,000 bowling alley built and paid for by the federal government. How did this happen?

In the 1990s, this community of less than two thousand people was a local headquarters for two hundred people working on a portion of the CUP project. They were certainly aiding the local economy, but local officials felt they weren't doing enough. According to the town manager, the town deserved cash assistance because the workers increased the town's expenses.

The town manager approached the Bureau of Reclamation about his idea for cash assistance. When rebuffed about getting cash, the town settled for something more tangible. "What about a recreational facility? What about a bowling alley?" The Bureau agreed.

With the tough decision made, the city and Bureau joined hands and approached their local congressman, Howard Nielsen, who supported the idea. He asked the Congressional Appropriations Committee for the money, and it complied. The committee instructed the Bureau to use "available funds" to build the bowling alley.

Word of the six-lane facility became public just before the grand opening. It was fodder for every major newspaper in the country, with articles appearing in the *Washington Post, New York Times, USA Today,* and hundreds of local papers. How many times does the federal government build a bowling alley for a local community?

The back-pedaling began almost immediately. The Bureau announced with some fanfare that they were going to get the water project beneficiaries to repay $281,000 of the total costs (presumably at zero percent interest over forty or more years).

When informed of this development, former Congressman Nielsen was not pleased, saying, "I thought they had money available in their budget. I would not have supported it had I known the money was going to have to be repaid." In other words, it was okay to stick the taxpayers with the bill, but not his constituents and certainly not the people using the facility.

This example is noteworthy for several reasons. First, it once again proves Congress is willing to spend taxpayers' money on almost anything related to a water project. Second, it shows that some members of Congress still think public money is free.

Third, and most important, it demonstrates an appalling lack of judgment and proper decision making by federal officials. Rather than simply carry out their legal mandate to build a water project, the federal officials decided they were free to agree with local officials to build a bowling alley. Congress and the public were never told of the bowling alley, and had they been, they would never have agreed to it.

Yet the federal officials involved felt free to accept the ludicrous arguments of local officials, lobby for authority to divert money to the bowling alley, and then oversee construction. No business plan. No economic analysis or cost-benefit analysis. Just a wink and a nod, and off they went.

———

The Bureau of Reclamation doesn't exist because it performs functions that can't be performed by other government or private entities. Rather, we keep this federal agency, with a budget of more than $1 billion a year, because it would be politically difficult for Congress to get rid of it.

But certainly it performs some function that no other organization can perform? Surely, something dramatic or catastrophic would occur if we abolished the agency?

The agency was established in 1902 because there was no repository of engineering construction expertise at the state or local level. If we were going to build large dams and canals to promote western settlement, we needed a group of people with the expertise to oversee these important construction projects.

Does the same problem exist today? Certainly not. State and local governments and private industry are perfectly capable of overseeing the construction of large water projects. They are already responsible for building the interstate highway system, sewage treatment plants, and a host of other infrastructure projects.

Well, maybe we need the Bureau to operate those large hydroelectric power-generating complexes? Afraid not. Hoover Dam was operated by employees of the Southern California Edison Company, an investor-owned utility, for the first fifty years of its existence. This state of affairs grated on Bureau employees and they successfully lobbied for an act of Congress to put federal employees in control of the powerhouse in the mid-1980s.

The same is true for all the other large power-generating facilities that the Bureau operates in the seventeen western states. Any number of other federal, regional, state, or local government organizations or the private sector is capable of operating these facilities.

What about operating and maintaining these complexes for

delivery of water to cities and farms? Isn't that a critical federal function that we need a separate agency to perform?

Not in my view. Turning the valves to release water is an easy task. Deciding when or if to turn the valve is more difficult, but certainly not overwhelmingly difficult. We delegate equally challenging tasks to state and local governments on a regular basis. This wouldn't be any different.

There have been disagreements between states along the Colorado River and other places throughout the West. These disagreements have almost led to open conflict in the past and they're the stuff of legends. (Arizona once called out its National Guard over a water dispute with California.) Surely, the federal government, acting through the Bureau of Reclamation, is needed to referee or settle these disputes?

Once again, I would say it's not necessary. Western states do disagree on issues, but they no longer call out the National Guard on each other. The worst that can happen is a protracted lawsuit, but they've seen enough of those; states will do just about anything to avoid them.

The nation has critical water problems and they're going to get worse. We need leadership to help address these issues. That leadership has traditionally come from our government institutions because they present the right forum and "neutrality" to debate and discuss how best to solve problems.

But how can we have leadership if our government institutions can't manage their finances, make thoughtful decisions, work with the Congress, comply with environmental laws, or address today's water problems? How can we have leadership if the only reason an agency exists is political expediency?

It is time we got rid of the Bureau of Reclamation.

Writing those words is painful to me because I spent more than two decades of my professional life trying to change the organization, working to make it better. But the obvious fact is that we don't need the agency any longer.

If we need to finance or build water projects, and the federal government wants to be involved, the federal government should provide the funds to state or local agencies to build them. If we want the federal government to generate electric power, deliver water to farms and cities, or implement environmental laws, there are entities other than the Bureau of Reclamation that can provide those services in better and cheaper ways.

No better proof of our need to eliminate the Bureau of Reclamation exists than another event that took place in Utah.

"You're not going to believe what the Bureau has done now," my co-worker said.

"Utah again?" I asked.

"Yep. Seems they've diverted $40 million in congressional add-on money intended for the CUP to finish some projects in Texas. Jake Garn is furious."

The first part of my co-worker's comment was not a surprise, but the second part was. While in office, former Senator Jake Garn of Utah had flown into space on the Space Shuttle and donated a kidney to his daughter who had diabetes. He was one tough character, and as a member of the Appropriations Committee, he was a ferocious protector of the CUP. He was not someone you wanted mad at you.

After the dust settled, we learned that the Bureau had indeed diverted the $40 million, and Senator Garn was hopping mad. To make matters worse, the Bureau had asked Garn the previous year to secure the money because they wanted to speed up construction on the project. After putting his credibility on the line and much arm-twisting, he was successful. But once they got the $40 million, Bureau officials changed their minds and decided to spend it in Texas—only they neglected to inform Garn.

The Bureau's inability to properly oversee the CUP, and especially their management of the finances, caused their supporters in Utah to conclude two things: the Bureau could not be trusted, and local officials could do a better job of managing project construction and finances.

When the $40 million intended for the project was diverted, it set in motion a series of events that resulted in an historic first: the Bureau of Reclamation was *fired* from constructing a federal water project. Fed up, the Utah congressional delegation led the effort to enact legislation to replace the Bureau with a five-member commission composed of Utah officials nominated by the President and confirmed by the U.S. Senate. The commission goes by the confusing name of the Utah Reclamation Mitigation and Conservation Commission. Their job was to oversee construction in cooperation with a three-person federal staff reporting directly to the secretary of the Interior. No bureaucracy, just a small commission staff and an even smaller contingent of federal employees auditing the books.

It is a unique experiment that worked. After more than two decades in existence, the commission has construction ahead of schedule and under budget. No bowling alleys are being built. No money is being diverted to Texas. No arguments are being heard about local officials not being involved.

Even environmental leaders are happy. The law establishing the commission also laid out a schedule of environmental mitigation projects to be constructed. In addition, the law mandates that environmental organizations be represented on the commission itself. The commission has adhered to the construction and mitigation schedule and water users and environmental leaders are pleased with the results.

If we abolished the Bureau of Reclamation, what is the proper role of the federal government in assisting in the solution of water problems? What is the federal interest? The agency itself recognizes that their future is shaky, and they're doing their best to paper over the problem. In 2005, they commissioned the National

Academy of Sciences to convene a panel on "the appropriate organizational, management, and resource configuration" to meet the agency's needs in the next century. The academy followed their instructions and issued a detailed report. The Bureau then issued forty-one action items and stated that it would take three years to study and implement. Today they are still studying the problem and mulling about their future.

Think of it this way. Here's a federal agency concerned about its relevancy in a modern, changing world. They've decided to take three years to figure out how they can be more relevant and timely, and take those three years to figure out how they can implement their ideas. Their approach was a classic bureaucratic response to a problem. When in doubt, don't make any decisions. Hire a consultant, issue a report, hold public hearings, create action plans and task forces, and generally ignore the recommendations until they are forgotten and out of the public's mind.

The problem with this approach (other than the ridiculous process it created) is that it fails to address the central question: Do we need a Bureau of Reclamation? The National Academy of Sciences was not asked to address that question and they didn't offer to pursue the subject. The agency itself has not asked that question and they never will.

Once again, this is not a problem associated with one political party or the other. The National Academy study was the brainchild of the George W. Bush Administration. When the Obama Administration came into office, they had the perfect opportunity to chart a new course. Armed with a new agenda and nearly a billion dollars of stimulus money, they had the mandate and funds to make a difference. They didn't.

The Obama Administration quietly plodded on allowing the Water Nobility to continue calling the shots. Like a ship without a helmsman or rudder, the Bureau of Reclamation continues to support the same tired approaches and to half-heartedly appear to be solving problems without actually doing so. They lack creativity, leadership, and a commitment to making a dent in solving western water policy issues.

———————

Every four years, the secretary of defense is required to undertake a review and issue a report with the tongue-twisting name of the "Quadrennial Defense Policy Review." Despite the cumbersome title, the review is a fascinating and useful document. The law that initiated the review directed the secretary of defense to examine some very fundamental questions, such as:

What kind of defense forces do we need for the near future?

Where should we concentrate our funding—on manpower, reserve forces, or weapons?

Is the Army too big or too small? Should we have large combat regiments or smaller, more mobile units?

Do the Navy and Air Force have the equipment they need to meet future defense threats? If not, what do they need and what will it cost?

What kind of conflicts should we anticipate fighting? Are we prepared to address these conflicts?

The review process and resulting report and recommendations are a useful exercise because it forces our leaders to question existing policies, anticipate future problems, and consider alternative approaches. It generates a useful national discussion about what the future holds and how we should address defense-related issues. Given the hundreds of billions of dollars we spend on national defense, this process is a necessary and appropriate way to have a national dialogue and shape future choices.

We should approach water issues in a similar way. It certainly makes more sense than a billion-dollar agency scurrying around for three years looking for a mission, the Water Nobility lobbying for more subsidies, or the Congress designating earmarks to please a few constituents.

We need to critically examine what the federal government

should be doing to help, how it can provide that help and what alternatives we have to provide the assistance. What kind of water issues will we encounter in the next decade or two? Are we prepared to address those challenges? If not, what changes do we need to make and why?

There are less than a handful of instances where a federal agency has been eliminated, even when there was good reason. But there is a compelling need to begin to address our water problems in a different manner, and we need leadership to do that. We certainly can't get that leadership from federal agencies that dream about the past and run in circles creating work for themselves.

I've come to the reluctant conclusion that you can't teach an old bureaucracy new tricks. If we want to address the water problems of the future in a different way, we need to start by eliminating out-of-date federal bureaucracies and create new processes that will ensure solutions to the problems of today and tomorrow.

5
Saving Them from Themselves

*An independent commission, not Congress,
should recommend the individual
water projects to be funded each year.*

I was in the office of former Idaho Congresswoman Helen Chenoweth who had been elected to Congress with the Republican Revolution of 1994. She had requested a meeting to discuss water problems associated with endangered salmon in the Snake River.

Mrs. Chenoweth had campaigned for Congress by opposing the Clinton Administration's federal land and water management policies. She had gained national attention when she held endangered salmon bakes and served canned salmon at campaign events to ridicule the Endangered Species Act.

Since winning her election, she never missed an opportunity to draw a distinction between her views and those of the administration. She quickly developed a reputation as a pit bull in high heels. On the few times I'd seen her in public, this reputation seemed to be well deserved.

That's what made this meeting so unusual. In the quiet of her office, she was pleasant, friendly, and charming.

I should have known better.

At the conclusion of our meeting, I left Capitol Hill and made the twenty-minute trip back to my office downtown. As I walked in, my assistant told me our regional director in Boise was calling.

"What did you say to Mrs. Chenoweth?" the director asked.

"Not much. We just discussed the problem in general terms, and it seemed to go very well. Why?" I replied.

"She issued a press release about an hour ago blasting you on the salmon recovery issue," he replied.

Ah, there's nothing like a member of Congress who issues a press release criticizing you *before* the meeting.

After their election to Congress, most politicians undergo an interesting ideological metamorphosis. They become mesmerized by the lure of spending federal money on water projects in their districts or states.

It doesn't matter what political party they belong to. Rather than being concerned about federal spending, conservative Republicans think more federal money should flow to their districts or states. Liberal Democrats suddenly begin chirping about the need for investments in their districts for jobs or to assist the business community. Members of Congress from both parties feel the more money the better.

Water issues give members of Congress a chance to show how they can perform for the folks back home. Their job is to get more money, loosen rules or regulations on how it is spent, and force officials to give their projects a higher priority.

Senator Bob Kerrey of Nebraska burst through the door like he'd been shot out of a cannon. He was an hour late for a meeting in central Nebraska to discuss a decision by one of my former employees to sign forty-year water contracts with several local irrigation districts. Only one problem: the employee didn't have the authority to sign the contracts, and he signed them the day he retired from federal employment.

My agency realized that we had a mess on our hands and we needed to clean it up quickly. All but one issue had been worked out before our meeting, and we had come to central Nebraska to resolve that issue with the local farmers. Senator Kerrey was here to lend his support to his constituents.

The moment he arrived, Senator Kerrey launched into a tirade against the federal government. He accused my agency and me of unfairly singling out his constituents. Didn't I know his constituents were providing food and fiber for the nation's dinner tables and our silly requirements were keeping them from their jobs? We were nitpicking, he said, and we needed to show more common sense. We needed to show some flexibility, not stick blindly to the letter of the law.

Senator Kerrey, a much-admired liberal Democrat, was putting on quite a show for his constituents.

There are unwritten rules associated with these kinds of government meetings. The senator had to establish that he was fighting for his constituents by publicly berating government officials, and demonstrate a working knowledge of the laws or regulations.

As the lead government official, my job was to appear to be listening intently and nodding at all the appropriate points. After the senator had a chance to impress everyone in the room, I was expected to compliment him on his persuasive case and offer a concession or compromise. The senator would then consider the offer, maybe even rub his chin to show great thought, and then turn to his constituents and say, "I think this is the best we're going to get. Can you live with this?" This was a signal the meeting was coming to an end.

The constituents were expected to reluctantly agree, and I was supposed to compliment the senator for bringing everyone together to find a constructive compromise. The next step was to meet with the press and let them know a resolution had been reached and, most importantly, make sure that they knew it was made possible by the direct involvement of the senator.

But in central Nebraska, things weren't going according to the script. Senator Kerrey was "off message" or, more accurately, he wouldn't stop talking. He was starting to believe his own rhetoric, and he was waving his arms about as if he were giving a speech to a large convention, but there were less than a dozen people in the room.

After what seemed like hours, I whispered to the senator's assistant that I had come to the meeting with a compromise, but since he was doing all the talking, I couldn't suggest it. She went around the table and whispered into the senator's ear. His eyes lit up, and without skipping a beat, said: "But enough of my views on this important subject. I'd like to know how the commissioner thinks we can solve this problem."

With that, we were back to the script. I offered the compromise, he thought for a second and turned to his constituents and suggested they accept the offer. They did, and that was the end of the meeting.

Our meeting in central Nebraska was just another performance from a long-running play that members of Congress perform year after year. This play might be entitled "The Pork Barrel Monologues." It is a play that has been running "off Broadway" for more than a hundred and fifty years, and it is time we brought down the final curtain.

The play begins with members of Congress deciding to become "champions" of a project in their home states or districts. Their role is to visit the site of a potential project and work with the local and federal officials involved to get the project authorized. The member of Congress then escorts local leaders to an out-of-town performance on Capitol Hill, where they make requests for funds and personally testify with the constituents before the committees who hand out the money for projects. And most importantly, a member of Congress gets to cut the ribbon when the project is completed.

Within Congress, it is the ultimate "I scratch your back you scratch mine" form of politics. The rules are very simple: "You don't question my project, and I won't question yours." Even when you know another member's project is idiotic and a waste of money, the unwritten rule is that you don't oppose the project. If your project or someone else's has clearly fictitious benefits or costs, you don't say anything. If a project is an environmental disaster, destroying endangered species, wetlands, or wildlife habitat, you just don't speak up.

What is the reward for your silence?

Other members of Congress will support your project, even though it may not be the best investment of federal dollars. You get a reward by staying silent or voting correctly when some maverick decides to buck the system.

In the criminal world, we call this behavior "bribery," but in the political world, it is called "good politics." Even though you know something is a waste of money or an environmental outrage, you look the other way, and you are rewarded.

The phrase "pork barrel" came into use as a political term in the post–Civil War era. It came from the plantation practice of distributing rations of salt pork to former slaves from wooden barrels. When used in Congress, it implies legislation loaded with special projects for members to distribute to their constituents as an act of largesse, courtesy of the taxpayers. This largesse doesn't serve the broader public interest; these are projects that serve a narrow constituency and provide benefits to only a few.

The results of this long-time practice would be funny if it weren't so serious. Congress repeatedly makes the same mistakes by directing money to members' pet projects and suffering well-deserved bad press for making inane decisions. One of the most famous was the "Bridge to Nowhere" in Alaska. The bridge would have connected Gravina Island, which contains Ketchikan International Airport and fifty residents, with the town of Ketchikan. This $400 million project was removed from federal legislation in 2005 after a huge public uproar, only to miraculously reappear as part of the 2011 transportation act.

When I was lobbying for the National Audubon Society, I remember asking a member of Congress with a strong environmental record to support an amendment reducing funding for a particularly disastrous project. I assumed he was a solid "yes" in our corner. His reply startled me: "Are you nuts? I've got a project in this bill, and if I vote for your amendment, they'll drop my project like a hot potato." The bill's authors had added deserving projects and projects that could only be described as "pork" to the bill. In this way, they squelch opposition to their bill, even securing the votes of members with sterling environmental records. That's the way the "system" works.

The Congress has authorized and funded uneconomic projects as special favors to scores of cities and towns and small select groups of farmers. They've funded projects that were environmental insults, projects that are wasteful expenditures of public funds, projects that didn't work, and projects that sit idle for years.

After the 2006 and 2010 elections, efforts were made by both the Democrats and Republicans in Congress to reform the system. "Earmarks" were banned and sincere efforts were undertaken to eliminate them. After the 2010 elections, Speaker of the House John Boehner made some long-overdue changes. He opposed earmarks and publicly urged restraint on federal spending. He downgraded the Appropriations Committee and made a genuine effort to eliminate earmarks. It was the most conscientious effort by a Speaker of the House in memory to control the appetite of members of Congress to spend in their districts.

Speaker Boehner was not doing this out of the goodness of his heart. He was responding to the pressure being applied by his new Tea Party–aligned majority. They wanted to rein in federal spending and he made a valiant effort to try.

He hasn't succeeded. Slowly, and inexorably, earmarks are working their way back into the system. Instead of blatantly directing federal agencies to spend money on a specific project, legislators now write more obtuse provisions that limit national programs in a way that means money can only be spent on one project, and that one project is in that member's district or state. Their other approach is to berate, hound, and arm-twist federal agencies into requesting funds for a project. Under the new rules, if an agency asks for a dam, canal, or tunnel, it isn't a congressional earmark.

As author Marc Reisner noted: "In the West, it is said, water flows uphill toward money. And it literally does ..." Over the last one hundred years, Congress has funded projects to dry up rivers, make rivers flow backward, diverted rivers from one drainage to another, made deserts blossom, and made productive farmland a lakebed.

Throughout the history of the western water program, Congress has supported some good projects and some bad ones. Unfortunately, the score is more heavily weighted on the negative side. But we can't judge success or failure based solely on what we consider appropriate in today's world. The cultural lens through which we examine projects has changed. What made sense in the middle of the Great Depression or World War II probably doesn't look like such a good idea today.

The important thing is for our leaders to make the best decisions possible based on the facts available at the time. Decisions should be based on thoughtful processes that carefully examine alternatives and ensure that we establish and meet clear national priorities.

Yes, politics will play a part, but it should not be the sole determinant as it is now. Under the current approach, priorities aren't established, alternatives aren't weighed, and thoughtful decisions aren't made. How could there be? The current system rewards blind allegiance to a quid pro quo system.

We need a better approach.

———

People have been trying to change the pork-barrel system for several decades, and they deserve an "A" for effort because they tried just about everything.

Every modern-day President has railed against pork-barrel spending by Congress and offered reforms to no avail. In the 1940s, President Roosevelt created a national planning board to guide government investments. It worked so well that Congress abolished the board because it was intruding upon congressional prerogatives.

In the 1950s, federal budget officials developed a system to analyze and compare the benefits and costs of water projects to encourage Congress to make more rational decisions. Everyone paid attention except Congress. They continued to approve projects whether they made economic sense or not.

In the 1960s, Congress established a federal agency to improve water project planning processes. Although well intended, it had no practical impact. Members of Congress didn't care whether projects were planned according to the best procedures; they went ahead with funding whatever they wanted.

President Jimmy Carter issued a list of water projects that he refused to continue funding. This "hit list" immediately (and permanently) injured his relationship with Congress. Members railed against this "insult," and in the end, Carter was only able to kill funding for less than a half-dozen projects.

The Congress loves to give the "appearance" of reforming the system. In 2006, the House of Representatives reached new heights in hypocrisy when it passed legislation giving the President line-item veto authority. This legislation allowed the President to go through funding bills passed by Congress and delete whatever earmarked or pork barrel expenditure he thought wasteful or inappropriate. Many governors have this authority and it has been on the wish list of budget-cutters for years.

Rather than reduce wasteful spending, this line-item authority legislation would have had the opposite effect. Since the President would now have the authority to delete wasteful spending, Congress would have no incentive to keep wasteful spending out of funding bills. They would be free to add one wasteful item after another and then blame the President if the items weren't deleted.

This proposal is the ultimate admission by the Congress that they can't control themselves. Rather than say "no" to a colleague's wasteful spending proposal, they would rather have the President do it. In a sense, Congress is asking the President to protect them from themselves.

Like most symbolic legislation, this one also died a quiet death because the Senate never acted on the bill and no subsequent Congress has since resurrected it.

––––––––

This history shows the lengths we have gone to end The Pork Barrel Monologues. Presidents, cabinet secretaries, reformers in Congress, and the advocacy community have spent lifetimes trying to change the system, with very little impact. The press delights in learning about the outrageous projects, and the public shakes their heads and says, "What can we do about it?"

Is there any hope to cure Congress of this addiction? Yes. There has been one similar case where Congress overcame its parochial nature and put the public interest above their own concerns—the closure of military bases.

In the 1980s, everyone agreed that we needed to close military bases and consolidate a number of military functions and activities. The Cold War was winding down and we had far too many bases in the wrong places. But closing bases was nearly impossible. The speaker of the House of Representatives certainly wasn't about to close a base or shipyard in his hometown. The majority leader of the Senate thought it was a good idea—as long as facilities in his state were spared. And so it went for every member of Congress. The result was that each year members of Congress complained that we had too many bases or shipyards, but they did nothing about it.

Then someone came up with a bright idea. Congressman Dick Armey was an unusual reformer. He was a recently elected member on the minority side of the aisle. That usually meant everyone ignored his ideas, but not this time. Armey suggested the creation of a Base Realignment and Closure Commission (BRAC) composed of nine independent members appointed by the President. They would receive a list of proposed base closings from the secretary of defense. They would visit the bases, meet with defense personnel, hold public hearings, and then develop a final closure list. This list would then be sent to the President, who had to accept or reject it in its entirety. Assuming he accepted the list, he would send it to Congress. They had forty-five days in which to pass a resolution of disapproval. If they didn't pass such a resolution, the recommendations would be considered final and the closures would take place.

The idea worked. Since the law was enacted in 1988, there have been six BRAC "rounds," which closed hundreds of bases and shipyards and significantly realigned our forces to meet more contemporary needs. In the process, we've saved hundreds of billions of dollars.

We need to undertake a similar approach for western water projects. The President should appoint a water project commission every five years, and they would solicit suggestions for projects from state and local governments, federal agencies, nonprofit institutions, and the general public. The commission would have six months to review the recommendations and come up with a set of water project priorities for the federal government to undertake during the following five years.

The commission's suggestions would be delivered to the President, who could accept or reject the list in its entirety. If he rejected it, the commission would have to go back and come up with another list.

Assuming the President agreed, the list would be sent to the House and Senate to be dealt with in the same manner as the military bases closure list. Like BRAC, no amendments would be allowed. Each chamber would be forced to accept or reject the entire list of recommended projects or let it go into effect. No earmarks. No side deals. No special favors.

It's time for a change. Establishing a water project commission would correct the worst abuses of the current system and treat the real addiction that affects members of Congress when it comes to water projects. Making these changes would result in real reform and save the U.S. Treasury—i.e., taxpayers—a great deal of money in the process.

6

Dams Aren't Forever

*We should remove unnecessary and environmentally
destructive dams to restore our rivers and streams,
and we should start with Glen Canyon Dam.*

We need to remove dams, not keep building them. But this is not a
popular notion in political circles.

No better example of this maxim exists than hearings held
by the House Resources Committee in 1997. The chairman of
the committee, former Congressman Jim Hansen of Utah, had
decided to hold a hearing on a proposal suggested by a handful
of environmentalists. Their suggestion was to drain the reservoir
behind Glen Canyon Dam (one of the largest man-made lakes in
America) and remove the dam, which is upstream from the Grand
Canyon. Mr. Hansen gave us a hint of his position on the issue in
his press release announcing the hearing when he said, "Personally, I think this is a bizarre idea."

By draining the reservoir, known as Lake Powell, and removing the dam, these forward thinking environmentalists saw that
we would be restoring a natural wonder—the magnificent Glen
Canyon—which rivals the Grand Canyon in its beauty, but had
been underwater since the mid-1960s when the dam was constructed. They also understood that this would improve management of Colorado River flows. But to Chairman Hansen, this was
a bizarre idea because Glen Canyon Dam and Lake Powell had
become permanent fixtures on the landscape.

From the opening gavel, there was no mistaking the intent of the hearing. The first few panels of witnesses firmly opposed draining the reservoir and they portrayed it as a ludicrous idea. Millions of people throughout the Southwest, they said, would experience water shortages and power failures if the lake were drained. Lake Powell tourism would collapse, and the economic impacts would be severe.

The few witnesses who were allowed to testify in support of the proposal to drain the reservoir were then brought before the committee. They were ridiculed by most of the western legislators as naïve, misguided, or worse. According to Dave Wegner, a former Bureau of Reclamation employee and river restoration advocate who was one the environmental witnesses that day, "It was a long, long hearing, and it wasn't a lot of fun."

But a strange thing happened on the way to the woodshed. By holding the hearing, the committee had given legitimacy to the most audacious dam-removal proposal ever suggested. It was now a national issue, rather than a dream in the hearts and minds of a handful of environmentalists.

The committee had not embarrassed their opponents—just the opposite. They had given their opponents a national stage to outline their plans and demonstrate that they were not a bunch of radicals, but a thoughtful group of experts who just might have a visionary idea.

Congressman Hansen did everyone a favor by holding these hearings. Even though he didn't mean to, the hearings proved that all it takes to remove dams and give us back our free-flowing rivers is political will. This hearing gave the issue of dam removal legitimacy, and it energized efforts to work for removing structures rather than building more of them.

———

The issue of dam removal is recent. It was sparked by the recognition that dams were having significant impacts on the physical environment. For decades, we perpetuated a myth that the adverse consequences of damming and engineering rivers were minimal and the benefits far outweighed any impacts.

More recently, some have advocated that dams and reservoirs are carbon-neutral and supply energy without negatively affecting climate change. This conveniently overlooks the destructive impacts that dams have on their immediate surroundings, their contribution to climate change, and climate impacts associated with the fuels and carbon needed to create the materials to build the dams. The carbon-neutral myth reached a new plateau in 2014 when Mark Tercek, the leader of America's largest environmental organization, The Nature Conservancy, said: "Environmentalists generally hate dams, even though they're clean energy."

Like high-pressure salesmen, those promoting dams, and their recent clean-energy apologists, have painted an ideal world: Cheap, clean, carbon-free power! Cheap water! Greater crop production! Economic development!

The reality is less rosy. Building a dam is a lot like constructing a nuclear power plant: you get immediate benefits, but you also get huge long-term costs. Just like a nuclear power plant, a dam can leave a legacy of environmental destruction that can take hundreds of years to correct. And dams take massive amounts of dirty energy to construct and to make the materials in the dam.

Dam projects built in the nineteenth and twentieth centuries, when viewed through the cultural lens of today, brought us only the illusion of progress. We have paid a huge price for our dam-building infatuation, and we'll continue to pay a significant price because dams have an impact on climate conditions.

We have spent billions of dollars for facilities that have become antiquated or, in some cases, don't work. We have inundated over 600,000 miles of streams and rivers, destroyed hundreds of thousands of acres of wetlands and other wildlife habitat. We have destroyed fish runs, eliminated fish species, increased salinity, degraded water quality, and destroyed wetlands. The number of major rivers in America that have *not* been dammed, dredged, or diverted can be counted on one hand. More than one-half of all the animals and plants on the endangered species list owe their precarious positions to water control structures.

And it's going to get worse. There's a growing body of science proposing that dams are a major contributor to climate change. Organic materials flowing into reservoirs decompose, emitting methane and carbon dioxide into the water and air. Dams drain and dry up downstream wetlands that are carbon sinks holding vast amounts of greenhouse gases in the soils.

For years, even the most ardent river protector or policy-maker didn't mention dam removal as an option. The advocacy group American Rivers has noted that dam removal, even up until the mid-1990s, only conjured up memories of Edward Abbey's characters' efforts to blow up Glen Canyon Dam in *The Monkey Wrench Gang*. Today, American Rivers lists a total of 1,150 dams that have been removed in the U.S., and that trend has increased sharply since the mid-1990s.

How and why did things change? It's hard to pinpoint one factor, but a number of events helped.

In 1992, Congress enacted legislation directing the removal of two dams on the Elwha River on the Olympic Peninsula in Washington state. This legislation, championed by former Senator Bill Bradley, was the first high profile dam-removal legislation enacted by Congress and served as a spark to ignite other efforts.

Twenty-five percent of all dams are now at least fifty years old and that number will rise to 80 percent by 2020, and the condition of most of these dams is poor. The insurance industry, which must cover any losses associated with dam failures, has started to pressure dam owners to fix them or take them down.

The Glen Canyon Dam hearings mentioned previously gave dam-removal proponents an important boost.

Finally, former Interior Secretary, Bruce Babbitt, did an excellent job of championing the issue in the 1990s. It certainly changes public opinion when a cabinet secretary gives speeches about tearing down dams and attends rallies with a sledgehammer.

Dam removal efforts in the past decade have attracted media attention and provided inspiration to a new generation of river advocates. The Edwards Dam on the Kennebec River in Maine was removed in front of television cameras with a dynamite explosion blowing a hole in the structure, and the image was replayed on national networks for several news cycles. The Elwha River dams were removed in an equally dramatic fashion and it has led to restoration of migratory salmon on the river.

In Wisconsin, community advocates working with state and local governments have made small dam removal the cornerstone of a statewide river restoration program. And so it goes in Pennsylvania, Virginia, Washington, and many other states across the nation. In 2012 alone, according to American Rivers, at least fifty additional dams were removed.

Dams move from the real world to the world of symbolism almost effortlessly. Once proponents decide a dam is needed, it seems to take on a life of its own. It becomes a symbol of progress, economic prosperity, and hope for the future. In other instances, dams become symbols of what a region thinks it is "owed." As a government official, more than once I've heard dam proponents say, "We were promised a dam by Washington, D.C. When we make promises, we keep them. Washington should do the same."

Even more interesting is that people are willing to blindly put their faith in the promise of a dam. Somehow, people see dams as a panacea for problems, both real and imagined. Even when you point out to someone that a dam won't solve their problems, they don't seem to want to hear it. They have somehow fixed their hopes on a mound of concrete and rebar stretched across a river, and they can't be dissuaded from the conclusion that this is the right approach and it will bring them a brighter future.

Because dams are so large, they look and feel permanent to most people. Once constructed and operating, a dam and reservoir cross an imaginary threshold and are brought easily into our lives. Something this large must be reckoned with, and we quickly make the necessary adjustments. We assume a large dam with a reservoir extending behind it is there permanently and we have to accept it. The dam and its reservoir are added to our language and maps and become a permanent part of our vocabulary and geography.

What most people don't realize is that dams and other structures are not permanent fixtures on the landscape. They are there because we made a political decision to build them. They didn't get there by accident. We made a conscious decision to invest money to build a dam, and that decision is always made by one of our political institutions. The decision to build a dam isn't a scientific decision or an economic one. It is, pure and simple, a political decision.

And it is also important to remember that dams don't last forever. Even though they appear on Google Maps or in a National Geographic atlas, that doesn't mean they are permanent. Dams can collapse, as the Teton Dam in Idaho did in the mid-1970s. Dams and reservoirs can fill with silt, and like any artificial structure, they will deteriorate with age. Most government regulators and insurance executives assume that the useful life of a dam is fifty to seventy-five years. After that, a decision must be made for safety reasons to rehabilitate the structure or remove it.

In many cases, the politicians who decided to construct a dam many years ago made mistakes. The problems a dam was built to solve sometime don't materialize or are resolved in other ways. A dam might be poorly designed or improperly constructed. For whatever reason, mistakes are made. In other instances, dams outlive their usefulness. We all make mistakes, and we all understand that an object can become obsolete. Times and conditions change.

Everyone accepts this reasoning up to the point where we begin to talk about removing dams. For some reason, when the suggestion is made that we should remove an obsolete or unnecessary dam, it is like lighting a match and tossing it on a stack of firewood soaked with gasoline—the explosion is immediate and intense.

It's quite reasonable for us to question that if a dam is no longer fulfilling its intended purpose whether it should remain standing. Our political institutions approve dam projects for a specific set of reasons at a particular point in time. After forty or fifty years, things change. Today, everyone would agree that we have a different economy, a different set of environmental values, and different social values than we did fifty years ago. If that's the case, why should we blindly accept and live with decisions made fifty or a hundred years ago if those are inconsistent with today's values or economy?

Even more compelling in my mind is this question: Why should we have to accept the misguided or mistaken decisions made by those who preceded us? Just because some politicians made a stupid decision fifty years ago doesn't mean we should have to live with their mistakes. Senator Barry Goldwater and Congressman Morris K. Udall both said late in their lives that Glen Canyon Dam had been a mistake and should never have been built. Why do we have to live with that mistake?

We have the ability to correct these mistakes. Just because the dam and reservoir are there and many perceive it to be a permanent fixture on the landscape doesn't mean it has to be. We can correct the mistakes of the past and make intelligent choices about the future.

———

When he announced the hearings on Glen Canyon Dam, Congressman Hansen offered a prediction. It was important to hold the hearing, he said, "so that the American people can understand just how extreme this proposal is and how it would impact millions of people ..."

How good was his prediction? Not very good.

Since those hearings were held, water supplies in the Colorado

River Basin have been in free-fall. The basin has gone through the most extreme drought in the past five hundred years. In 2000, Lake Mead and Lake Powell were nearly full. After the driest fifteen-year period in the Colorado River Basin in the last one hundred years, both reservoirs are now half empty, and the "bathtub rings" around each reservoir are a constant reminder of the impact of this extended drought.

The lack of rain was not the only reason lake levels dropped. The Bureau of Reclamation, egged on by its customers, bet that the drought would end and rainfall would return to "normal." It was a calculated gamble that didn't pay off. In an ironic twist, the insatiable greed of the Water Nobility and the "never say no" attitude of federal agencies combined to drain Lake Mead and Lake Powell to levels even the environmentalists couldn't have imagined.

In addition, in 2000 an important milestone was reached when the supply and demand requirements in the Colorado River Basin intersected. Up to 2000, there was always a supply buffer somewhere in the system that could be called upon to meet the needs of an area in drought. After 2000, the water buffer (except for the water in the reservoirs) was gone, and as demand continued to grow, the existing supply no longer could meet demand. There was no extra water in the system to handle a long-term drought, and risks in the system increased considerably.

Federal, state, and local officials are scurrying around in a near panic as they see water levels dropping and the prospects for future rainfall more and more remote. Studies of how to "augment" supplies, re-operate facilities to squeeze out more water, and other supply enhancements have become the obsession of federal and state officials. There is now real concern that both reservoirs could drop to levels where the production of power would be inhibited, and the delivery of water to downstream users curtailed. Deliveries to Las Vegas, for example, come directly from Lake Mead, and as the lake levels have dropped, officials have become concerned that water levels could drop below the city intake.

And the prospects for the future don't look good. University of Washington scientists predict the flow of the Colorado River to decline by one-third by 2050. Researchers at the University of California–San Diego's Scripps Institution of Oceanography predict that there is a 50 percent chance that by 2036 Lake Mead could drop to "dead pool" status, meaning that no water would be able to be released downstream.

The short-term prospects are equally bleak. If drought conditions persist, there is a significant probability that by 2016 federal officials will have to declare a shortage and drastic reductions in supplies to Arizona and Nevada would ultimately ensue. In the summer of 2014, the elevation of Lake Powell was ninety-four feet below full pool and only 51 percent of full capacity. The "most probable" Bureau of Reclamation estimates show a continuation of current lake levels through 2016.

Rather than look upon this situation as a doom-and-gloom exercise, the fifteen-year drought and the dim prospects for water supplies from Lake Mead and Lake Powell present us with an opportunity to implement a bold and innovative approach. We should drain Lake Powell, remove Glen Canyon Dam, and allow the Colorado River to keep Lake Mead full.

Glen Canyon Dam has reached the end of its useful life. The dam and reservoir were justified to Congress in the 1950s as the perfect solution to water supply uncertainty for the fast-growing Southwest. The dam and reservoir, it was thought, would store water to help upper basin states meet their water delivery requirements. It would regulate floods, and it would generate cash to finance future water development in the upper basin states through the sale of electric power.

But after fifty years, it is now apparent that Glen Canyon Dam and Lake Powell are far from the perfect solution to the region's water problems.

The dam was built for mistaken political reasons as Senator Goldwater and Congressman Udall admitted. It was built to help the upper basin states of Colorado, Wyoming, Utah, and New Mexico meet their water delivery requirements under the Colorado River Compact. However, saying that these delivery requirements were the driving force behind the construction of Glen Canyon Dam is a "red herring." It's a specious argument used by the upper basin states to justify the unjustifiable. No one from the four upper basin states will go to jail if their delivery requirements are not met. If the river doesn't have the water, there's little anyone can do to force the upper basin states to send more water down the river.

The real reason the upper basin states wanted Glen Canyon Dam was to store water so electricity could be sold and revenues potentially could be used for future water development. The law authorizing Glen Canyon Dam stated that revenues from the sale of power would be put into an Upper Colorado River Basin Fund and could be available for future projects—with one important caveat. The law states that while hydropower revenues will be "credited" to the fund, the money actually goes into the General Receipts of the U.S. Treasury and is used by Congress for whatever it wants. The Basin Fund revenues can't be used for water project development without an act of Congress. Despite this reality, the upper basin states feel that as long as they can point to an account in the treasury with plus numbers, they've got a chance of getting the federal government to pay for future water development projects.

Glen Canyon Dam has often been referred to as a "savings account" for Lake Mead. Water would be stored behind Glen Canyon Dam and sent down to Lake Mead when it was needed. But with lake levels dropping, the savings account is now half-empty and there is every prospect that the account will be overdrawn in the next decade.

The proponents of Glen Canyon Dam knew it would not serve as a water supply facility. No water is withdrawn from Lake Powell for farmers or cities. The only water that leaves the reservoir is used to generate electric power, piped to the Navajo Generating Station (a coal-fired power plant) for cooling purposes, or it evaporates from the reservoir surface. The evaporation is significant. Lake Powell, because of its high desert location and huge surface area, loses an average of 860,000 acre-feet[1] of water annually to evaporation and bank seepage. This is enough water to meet the yearly water requirements of the city of Los Angeles. In fact, Lake Powell loses more than 6 percent of the Colorado River's annual flow through evaporation and bank seepage.

Historically, the most important justification for Glen Canyon Dam is to serve as a peaking power facility to supply instantaneous demand for electric power to southwestern cities and towns. This ability for peaking power has diminished considerably since the 1990s, when restrictions were put on dam operations to protect endangered fish and beaches in the Grand Canyon, downstream of the dam.

There is no doubt Glen Canyon Dam has been a cash register power station. The installed capacity of the power plant is 1,320 megawatts of power. But the actual production depends on how much water is available to produce power. The output has varied from a high of 10.4 billion kilowatt hours (kW) in 1984 to less than 2 billion kW in 2002. The current average is 5 billion kW.

These are substantial numbers, but it is important to understand that there are alternatives to replace this power, although replacement power would not likely be made available at the subsidized rates afforded the current customers of Glen Canyon Dam power.

The debate over power production at Glen Canyon could be a very short one. If lake levels continue to drop as the experts have predicted, the Bureau of Reclamation will not be in a position to produce any power because the lake levels will be below the intakes

---

[1] "Acre-feet" is the measure most commonly used to describe water delivered for agricultural, industrial, or commercial purposes. It is the amount of water required to cover an acre of land, one foot deep. This is 325,851 gallons, or enough water to meet the needs of four people for one year.

for the power generating facilities. When the reservoirs drop to within fifty feet of the generator intakes, air begins to be entrained in the water, which will cause cavitation in the turbines. This will lead to turbine failure and potentially catastrophic situations.

The current state of affairs at Glen Canyon Dam leads me to conclude that we should remove Glen Canyon Dam, drain Lake Powell, and allow the Colorado River to fill Lake Mead behind Hoover Dam. Constructing the dam was an historic blunder of monumental proportions and based on a false set of assumptions. It was the product of political wheeling and dealing, and today we are stuck with a half-empty reservoir that evaporates nearly a million acre-feet of water into the atmosphere. The upper basin states cling to the hope that someday, somehow, they will be able to use "free" federal dollars collected from electricity sales to build dams in their states.

In the meantime, this reservoir continues to flood a canyon that is one of America's natural wonders. John Wesley Powell described it as a land of beauty and glory, and Edward Abbey wrote that Glen Canyon was a portion of earth's original paradise. They were both right. To visit Glen Canyon is to undergo an awe-inspiring experience. It is truly a magical place and to continue to flood this natural wonder is a crime of monumental proportions.

When will common sense take hold? We are locked in a multi-decade drought and we have two half-empty reservoirs and it is doubtful both reservoirs can or will ever refill. Rather than cling to the past or tinker at the margins, we should chart a new course, a course that will improve power production from Hoover Dam and provide more reliable water supplies for the Colorado River.

I recognize the political infeasibility of draining Lake Powell and removing Glen Canyon Dam. But someone has to point out the obvious and begin advocating for sanity. If we do nothing, lake levels will continue to drop and water supplies to some of America's largest cities could be curtailed. Power production will be threatened. Water will continue to evaporate. And a priceless canyon—"a land of beauty and glory"—will remain hidden.

If we do nothing and allow nature to take its course, the Water Nobility will likely concoct another multi-billion dollar proposal that will pick our pockets and only offer Band-Aid solutions.

Removing dams makes economic and environmental sense. Removing Glen Canyon Dam makes the most sense of all. We need to begin the dialogue about why and how to remove this obsolete structure.

7

Declare Victory and Withdraw

*The federal government should terminate its involvement
with the largest irrigation district in California.*

When it comes to water, California is one of the most unique places on earth.

Almost two-thirds of the state gets less than twenty inches of rainfall each year, and this rainfall comes mainly in the winter. Over the past thirty years, Fresno, Los Angeles, and San Francisco all *averaged* less than 0.2 inches of rain for the entire summer. That's less than one small thunderstorm in the rest of the country.

To tourists, California doesn't look like a semi-arid desert. Green lawns, shrubs, and trees are everywhere. But this green veneer hides a secret. As the writer Marc Reisner observed, "California, which fools visitors into believing it is 'lush,' is a beautiful fraud." The fraud is made possible by water.

Californians store and move water around the state on a scale unparalleled anywhere else on earth. They move water hundreds of miles from where it falls as rain or snow to places where it is needed—or assumed to be needed. Most of the state is covered with an elaborate plumbing system that moves enough water to meet the needs of thirty-eight million people. (If it were a country, it would be the thirty-third largest in terms of population, larger than Canada.) California also moves enough water to sustain the tenth most productive economy in the world and the most productive agricultural economy in the United States.

In the Central Valley, California's plumbing is at its most intricate and interesting. The Central Valley extends 475 miles from Redding in the north to Bakersfield in the south. That's the distance between Boston and Washington, D.C. Clouds coming off the Pacific Ocean dump rainfall and snow on the western side of the Sierra Nevada Mountains. Rivers and streams flow off the Sierras and join to form the Sacramento River, draining the northern half of the valley, and the San Joaquin River, draining the southern half. These two rivers meet halfway between the north and south points at the delta of the Sacramento and San Joaquin Rivers and then flow into San Francisco Bay.

The plumbing system required to distribute water around the state is a hodge-podge of local, state, and federal dams and canals. In the case of the federal Central Valley project, water is stored behind dams in the north and released into the Sacramento River. The water flows south some two hundred miles, irrigating farms along the way. When it reaches the delta of the Sacramento and San Joaquin Rivers, an almost unimaginable engineering feat takes place. Enough water to meet the needs of thirty-eight million people for a year is pumped through the delta and put into the Delta-Mendota Canal. Then it is sent another hundred and fifty miles south and *uphill*, where it irrigates the largest irrigation district in America—the Westlands Water District.

The federal government became a major player in California's plumbing system by accident. The Central Valley Project had been started by the state, but when the bond market collapsed in the early 1930s, there was no way to proceed. The Bureau of Reclamation, armed with federal dollars, stepped in and began to plan and construct projects. They soon became involved in a bureaucratic race that is still hard to comprehend.

The Corps of Engineers and the Bureau dueled with one another, staking out dam sites up and down the Central Valley, lining up supporters and pursuing construction activities at an astonishing pace. The Bureau built the Shasta, Folsom, and Friant Dams. The Corps countered with major dams on the Kings, Kern, Kaweah, and New Melones Rivers. It was a bizarre battle pitting the egos of water bureaucrats and military engineers, aligned with their congressional patrons and local sponsors, staking out rivers and pouring concrete in a helter-skelter pattern that made little sense. This was not responsible resource development, it was an ugly bureaucratic turf war.

The state of California, not to be outdone, got into the act in the 1960s. They built the State Water Project, which stores water seventy miles north of Sacramento. The water is then sent down river, through the delta, and south nearly five hundred miles to Los Angeles. As a reminder of the turf wars, both the state and federal canals make their way through the San Joaquin Valley within a stones throw of one another.

The amount of water moved by these two parallel plumbing systems is amazing. Together they carry enough water to meet the annual water needs of more than eighty million people. When you fly over the valley and see the canals snaking their way across the landscape, you can't help but marvel at these engineering achievements. It's hard to visualize the length of these canals. If you put just the main river channel and canal delivery systems of the state and federal projects south of the delta end-to-end, they would stretch 1,660 miles, farther than the distance from New York to Houston or Chicago to Miami.

———

Without water storage and water conveyance, the California we know would not exist.

The ego, vision, and politics that enabled California's water system to be developed left considerable wreckage in the aftermath. The environment of the Central Valley, once a lush and productive grassland and marsh, was transformed into a flat, treeless landscape with farmland as far as the eye can see. Fisheries were destroyed as rivers were dammed or diverted. Wetlands were drained and wildlife habitat destroyed. Taxpayers were forced to provide subsidies from the state and federal treasuries to fuel the growth.

But the transformation also made winners, and the biggest winners of all were the farmers served by the federal project. The Central Valley Project is the greatest water gift any group of farmers in America has ever received. Half of the irrigated acres served by the federal government are in California. When you combine the $3.6 billion spent on dams and canals with the interest subsidy, debt forgiveness, and cheap power, these lucky California farmers are provided with a competitive advantage worth tens of billions of dollars.

But our gift was not distributed evenly. There were winners, and then there were really big winners—the six hundred farming operations that make up the Westlands Water District.

The water district was the last unit of the Central Valley Project to be built, and water was first delivered in 1963. Westlands, a public agency created under California state law, currently has contracts with the federal government for delivery of 1,150,000 acre-feet of water annually, and this water is required to be delivered to them at rock-bottom prices, cheating the federal treasury (and taxpayers) of revenues that they should be receiving. By one conservative estimate, the *yearly* water subsidy to the district of up to $110 million is the most profitable arrangement for any water district in America. The subsidy results from the zero interest loans for capital costs, deferring repayment of those costs, and the difference in the price farmers pay for the water and the price the taxpayers could receive for that water if it was sold on the open market. In essence, they've been given a payment or price break worth up to $110 million each year.

Stop and think a minute about this figure. Every year, we give up to $110 million in the form of a water subsidy to the six hundred farm operations in the district. It is theirs to do with what they want. It is a gift from us taxpayers to them; no strings attached. We gave it to them last year, we gave it this year, and we'll continue to give it every year until we decide to stop. That's like writing a check to each of the six hundred farms in the district for $183,000 every January first.

Just who receives these subsidies? The recipients are a small group of elite farming operations. Some are real farms, others are "paper farms." This means a large farming operation of several thousand acres that is operated as one enterprise, but on paper, it appears to be several smaller farms each 960 acres or less in size. In this way, the operations can avoid paying a higher price for the federal water they receive.

The Environmental Working Group analyzed farm and water data and calculated how much each member of Westlands received from taxpayers ten years ago. The winners were fifteen farming operations that received an annual water subsidy in excess of $1 million. Topping the list was Woolf Enterprises, which received a subsidy of between $3.5 and $4.2 million per year. Dresick Farms, Inc. received $2.3 million in subsidies, Vaquero Farms, $2.1 million, and so on down to Borba Brothers Farms, Terra Linda Farms II, and Westside Harvesting L.P., which received a paltry $1.1 million each.

When this subsidy analysis was announced, Stuart Woolf, president of Woolf Enterprises, first disputed the number, saying the subsidy was no more than $500,000. He pointed out that his 20,000-acre enterprise, which he said consists of a collection of 960-acre farms owned on paper by members of his family, was surviving by economies of scale, not subsidies. Disappointed in the lack of support he felt farmers were receiving, Mr. Woolf lamented that if he were starting out to be a farmer today, "I would go to Brazil."

Let's make sure we understand what is going on here. Federal taxpayers provide a subsidy each year for the water Mr. Woolf and his family must have to stay in business. Everyone agrees the subsidy is substantial, somewhere between $500,000 and $4.2 million. Woolf Enterprises has created a series of paper farms to give the appearance of complying with a federal law limiting subsidies, and he openly runs these paper farms as one operation, getting the largest water subsidy provided to any farm in the nation. He's disappointed, however, because "it seems as though agriculture no longer enjoys a strong public commitment ..." He's so disappointed that, if he had to do it over again, he'd go to Brazil.

The Bureau of Reclamation had a unique opportunity to correct this giveaway when it renegotiated the water supply contracts with Westlands in the period 2001–2007. Unfortunately, it failed to make any progress toward reducing the subsidy or reducing the amount of water that the Bureau agreed to deliver. The new twenty-five-year contract that the Bureau negotiated (which has an automatic twenty-five-year renewal clause)·would commit the federal government to delivering over one million acre-feet. The contract is awaiting final approval pending resolution of several legal issues.

But there's one small problem. The Bureau of Reclamation currently doesn't have enough water to meet the needs of farmers in Westlands and the rest of the Central Valley Project, plus meet their obligations to endangered species and local cities in California. Why did they commit to deliver more to Westlands for the next twenty-five or fifty years? One reason is to force the taxpayers to support construction of new storage and conveyance facilities worth billions of dollars because they will be "contractually obligated" to deliver water to Westlands. The current canal system is at capacity and the Bureau would have an excuse to be in charge of building new facilities.

And if the Bureau developed and delivered the new water, how would the farmers drain this water off their fields? If irrigation water isn't drained off fields, salts build up and the land is unable to grow crops. The Bureau has struggled for fifty years to find a solution to this problem to no avail. It originally thought that it would build a drainage canal and dump the water in the delta, but that proved infeasible when delta water districts objected to having contaminated drainage water dumped on their doorstep. It also looked at piping the drainage to the ocean, but coastal communities objected to that.

The Westlands Water District's latest effort to "solve" the drainage problem is to file a billion dollar claim in the U.S. Court of Claims in Washington, D.C. and hire one of the nation's most well-connected law firms to plead their case that the drainage problem belongs to the Bureau. But as of yet, the Bureau of Reclamation, or anyone else for that matter, hasn't found a solution to the drainage problem even though the federal government continues to commit to deliver more water.

The recent drought has thrown a curveball at Westlands and the Bureau of Reclamation. Even though Westlands had signed overly generous contracts to deliver water, the Bureau has not been able to deliver a consistent supply of water. In 2006, water deliveries to Westlands were at 100 percent and then dropped to 50 percent the next year. In 2009, deliveries dropped to 10 percent, but rose to 80 percent in 2011. In 2014, the Bureau announced that no federal water would be delivered to Westlands. Since Westlands was the last district to sign contracts, they are the first district to be "shorted" when drought conditions prevail.

Westlands farmers have had to make some significant changes in operations to adjust to the drought and more inconsistent water deliveries. They have converted to higher value crops, pumped more groundwater, fallowed some fields, and purchased expensive water on the open market.

Westlands Water District hasn't sat idle during these chaotic times. Reduced water supplies have prompted them to ramp up their lobbying efforts. In 2013, the Westlands Water District couldn't make it rain in California, but they certainly could in Washington, D.C. They spent $600,000 on lobbying efforts (six times their normal rate) in an effort to get legislation passed to force more water to be delivered and provide compensation to their operations for the drought. Despite their best efforts, no legislation was passed.

The debates surrounding the Westlands Water District seem to be never-ending. Despite generous federal water subsidies, the district carries on a continual fight to get the U.S. taxpayers to pay for solving their drainage problems, and they spend lavishly on lobbying and legal fees to secure even more water. All this money and effort just to appease six hundred farms in the wealthiest irrigation district in America. And the payments don't stop there. Westlands farmers also receive tens of millions of dollars in conservation, disaster, commodity, and crop insurance subsidies through the U.S. Department of Agriculture.

This is our federal bureaucracy at its bumbling best. Our public servants are intentionally promising to deliver more water than they know they can deliver so they can come to Congress to ask for help to fulfill their overblown promises. Members of Congress, always willing partners in such ventures, will start to give speeches about the need to build these projects because the federal government has made a "commitment" to provide this water, and we need to help meet the food and fiber needs of our nation. In the meantime, the six hundred paper farms that will be the beneficiaries of this largesse will continue to pocket their subsidies and complain that they need more.

———

How did we get ourselves into this mess? How did the Westlands Water District so adroitly pick our pockets?

Over the past fifty years, Westlands has used lobbyists, lawyers, campaign contributions, and electoral politics to control the Bureau of Reclamation program in California. They have reshaped the national program. They have been tough, astute negotiators and political activists. They have relentlessly worked the "system" to achieve their own parochial interests. This hasn't been by accident.

Westlands' long-time general manager, Tom Birmingham, made these observations in one of its annual reports: "In forging fertile fields from arid ground and in diligently remaining ahead of the constant changes that confront agriculture, Westlands has at times strongly asserted the legal and political rights of its users. The positions the District has taken have not always been the easiest, however, true leaders are often called upon to make difficult decisions and take unpopular steps."

Westlands has not only been unpopular, they have consistently been more strategic, more cunning, and more clever than the federal government or their critics. They have outmaneuvered and outlasted their adversaries at every turn.

When the federal government ordered Westlands to comply with acreage limits, the farmers in Westlands invented paper farms. When the press exposed this violation of the law in the 1970s and 1980s, Westlands threw up its hands and said the law needed to be changed. Then they invested millions of dollars in lobbying expenses and got the law changed so it suits their needs.

When Westlands wanted to increase its size by 100,000 acres to provide subsidies to more farmers, they did it despite a law saying they couldn't. The district simply got the top Interior Department lawyer to re-interpret the law. Coincidentally, before rendering this opinion, the official was a partner in a law firm representing large farming interests in the Central Valley.

When presidential candidates, whether Democratic or Republican, need to raise money in California, Westlands is a mandatory stop on the circuit, with the farmers at the front of the line writing checks. In the period 2010–2014, for example, the Westlands Water District spent a reported $1.6 million on federal lobbying activities. Westlands board members contributed an additional $200,000.

When elected leaders, Democratic or Republican, fail to support Westlands' positions, they are opposed and usually defeated at the next election. When federal employees sit down with Westlands on any issue, they know they're at a disadvantage because if they push too hard, they'll pay with their jobs. When an impasse is reached with a federal official, Westlands quickly files suit in Fresno Federal District Court. This ensures a sympathetic judge and has the added advantage of delaying a decision until they can get a sympathetic federal official to give them the right answer.

When a friendlier President is elected, Westlands enters into negotiations to settle their lawsuits. To the surprise of no one, Westlands reaches an out-of-court settlement that guarantees they will continue to get more water at a cheap price for a longer period.

Former NBA star and Senator Bill Bradley of New Jersey related a charmingly naïve story about money, politics, and Westlands in his book *Time Present, Time Past.* His first trip to the Central Valley was in 1982, when local Congressman Tony Coelho hosted several fund-raisers for Bradley's 1984 Senate campaign. "I had not put two and two together," Bradley wrote. "I was naïve enough to think that the contributors must like basketball." But those who came to the event, Bradley ultimately learned, "were the water boys, gaining what they hoped was a little insurance on the vote of a new, eastern member of the Energy and Natural Resources Committee." In this case, trying to buy some "insurance" backfired when Bradley became a catalyst for reform in California water politics.

The pursuit of influence also extends to those whom Westlands hires to assist them. As one blogger observed, "Who you know and who you pay is more important than what you know." Westlands has been very strategic in who they hire to provide lobbying, consulting, or connections. In 2011, two months after he retired from the bench, former federal judge Oliver Wanger agreed to represent Westlands in a state court matter. He did so even though Westlands had appeared before him as a plaintiff or defendant in numerous lawsuits over the previous decade.

It doesn't stop there. After the 2008 election, Westlands strategically added a new law firm to its brain trust—the firm of Brownstein Hyatt Farber and Scheck of Denver. Over the past two presidential administrations, lawyers in the firm have played a role in influencing national water policy. President George W. Bush's Interior Secretary, Gale Norton, was a partner at Brownstein before joining the cabinet. Ken Salazar, Obama's Interior secretary, owed his political career to the firm. They managed his successful campaigns for Colorado State attorney general and U.S. Senate, the positions he held before joining the Obama cabinet.

Westlands is the poster child for a federal program gone awry. Their relentless pursuit of more subsidies, more water, and more favors has tainted every federal official who has tried to enforce the law or do what makes common sense. They have given the entire western water program a black eye. The public perception is that Westlands *is* irrigated agriculture.

Their excesses have been held up to public scrutiny and ridiculed in the press. Newspapers have undertaken investigations and won prizes for the resulting stories. They have been the subject of television exposés and award-winning books. The General Accountability Office has conducted investigations, and the Interior Department Inspector General has written critical reports. Congressional oversight hearings have been held, and laws targeted to specifically control their abuses have been enacted.

Yet nothing seems to head them off course. Westlands plows ahead like a stubborn mule, confident that they will get their way.

For more than forty years, I have participated in repeated efforts to find ways to control Westlands' excesses and bring some sanity to this mess. In 1992, I worked with Congressman George Miller and Senator Bill Bradley to help develop and enact the Central Valley Project Improvement Act. This comprehensive legislation initiated water contract reforms, raised prices for water, established a fund financed by farmers to correct past environmental damage, promoted fish and wildlife restoration, and mandated a wide range of other reforms.

But the 1992 reforms haven't been enough. Westlands has methodically beaten back most of the provisions, and with the help of their friends in the George W. Bush Administration and the acquiescence of the Obama Administration, their prospects for success grow larger every day.

This state of affairs reached a new low in 2006 when the *New York Times* reported that the lead official negotiating the Westlands contract renewal was formerly a paid advocate for Westlands and other Central Valley farmers. The official, then Deputy Assistant Secretary of Interior Jason Peltier, had been the executive director of the Central Valley Project Water Association for the ten years prior to his appointment with the Bush Administration. As the head of the association, he was a forceful lobbyist and advocate who wasn't shy about promoting the best interests of his members.

When he first joined the Bush Administration in 2001, Mr. Peltier properly recused himself from working on California water issues. But things didn't stay that way for long. "I was given dispensation early on because of my knowledge of these issues," he said.

Bush Administration officials tried to smooth over the problem. Assistant Secretary Mark Limbaugh, Mr. Peltier's boss, maintained that his deputy was only providing background, insight, and advice. "He is not in a position to make the ultimate decisions," Limbaugh noted. When asked about his role in the contract negotiations, Mr. Peltier said, "I've tried to steer away from the nuts and bolts" of the contract.

Larry Noble, executive director of the Center for Responsive Politics, captured the essence of this scam when he said: "It is one thing to have someone with a certain ideological bent fill a political position, but it's another to have somebody who is so identified with a special interest that they cannot be expected to make fair decisions." What happened? The new contracts were signed in 2007 and are still the subject of litigation. And where is Jason Peltier today? He's now the chief deputy general manager at the Westlands Water District.

The insatiable greed of the six hundred farm operators in Westlands is never-ending. No matter how much money and water we pour into their district, it won't be enough. They will come back with their hand out for more. And why not? The federal government has a consistent record of agreeing (or capitulating) to their outrageous requests.

Enough is enough. Here's a very simple solution. Let's cut them free of the federal tentacles. We should declare victory and withdraw, as former governor and senator George Aiken of Vermont suggested as a way to end U.S. involvement in the Vietnam War. There is no reason why the federal government, especially the federal taxpayer, needs to continue to pour money into this venture. Congress made a decision to get us involved, and they can make a decision to get us out.

Westlands is the largest irrigation district in America, led by savvy leaders who are perfectly capable of existing on their own. If Westlands wants more water in the future, let them build the facilities to store the water, deliver it to their lands, and drain it off their fields. The federal taxpayers are under no obligation to assume this responsibility. The Westlands Water District can figure out how to do this without using our checkbooks. We're only involved because of historical accidents and the blind ambition of some unnamed federal bureaucrats and long deceased politicians who were participants in an insane turf war.

When examined from the perspective of today's environmental and fiscal realities, the continued involvement of the federal government in Westlands doesn't make any sense. Whether it was the right or wrong decision in 1961 is immaterial. We shouldn't invest one additional taxpayer dollar in this project.

8

Wrap It in an Indian Blanket

*Settlement of Indian water rights claims should not
be used as an excuse to build uneconomic
water projects or fleece the taxpayers.*

"Why not wrap it in an Indian blanket?" That's what my counterpart on the Senate subcommittee said to me when I was the staff person in charge of hearings on the need for a rural water supply system in western South Dakota.

For three straight years, we had the same hearings where the same witnesses described the same problems and read the same testimony on the same issue. The problem was genuine, but the solution seemed intractable.

The land west of the Missouri River in South Dakota is beautiful yet inhospitable. The people who settled this land were a tough and independent people, scratching out a modest living, primarily through ranching, in small towns and rural homesteads located considerable distances from one another.

This part of South Dakota also played a very cruel joke on the residents of West River. Located close to one of the largest rivers in North America, residents had little useable water supplies. The surface water was undrinkable because it was contaminated with dissolved minerals, radium, and fluoride. The only drinking water came from very deep wells (between 1,200 and 4,000 feet deep), and even that water was highly contaminated, looking like watered-down molasses.

The West River folks turned for help to their congressional

delegation in the late 1980s. The delegation introduced a bill directing the secretary of the Interior to build a treatment plant and pipeline, but the chances of getting the bill enacted were slim to none.

I sat in the hearing room, listening to the witnesses from West
River plead their case for the third straight year. As always, the
highlight of their presentation was to hold up a large jar of contaminated water from one of their ranches and then proceed to
pass it around to each member of the subcommittee. The members
of Congress would always turn up their noses, shake their heads,
and express great sympathy for the West River folks.

The problem was how to write legislation that would pass a
straight-face test. This meant we needed to write a bill that could
withstand scrutiny from legislators from other regions of the
country who would ask: "Why should my constituents pay for a
$100 million treatment plant and distribution line for a few thou-
sand rural residents of South Dakota? If we do it for South Dakota,
why can't we do the same for my constituents?"

This is where the "Indian blanket" became critical. To the east
and west of the affected counties were the Lower Brule Indian Reservation and the northeastern portion of the Pine Ridge Indian
Reservation. Both reservations suffered the same water contamina-
tion problems as their non-Indian neighbors in West River. Problems on the reservations were made even more pronounced by the
crushing poverty, poor housing, and social welfare and education
problems affecting the residents. Shannon County, home to the Pine
Ridge Reservation, is almost always ranked as the poorest county in
America, and the Lower Brule Reservation isn't far behind.

The federal government's relationship with Indian tribes is
unique and fascinating. It began during the French and Indian
Wars when the British signed treaties with tribes to enlist them to
fight against the French. When the United States was formed, we
honored those treaties and continued to sign new ones with various tribes.

Through a series of early Supreme Court cases and executive

actions, the relationship between Indians and the federal government was laid out. In three cases heard before the Supreme Court between 1823 and 1832, Chief Justice John Marshall ruled that Indians were "wards" of the federal government, which was responsible for their health, welfare, and education. Moreover, only the federal government, not the states, had jurisdiction over tribes and individual Indians. Over time, the concepts laid out in those cases established that the federal government had a trust relationship with federally recognized Indians and tribes. This relationship was similar to that of a trust department at a bank that is responsible for protecting the assets of a trustee.

What this meant for the Lower Brule and Pine Ridge Reservations was that the federal government had a responsibility to help them meet their water supply needs. Even more important, it is an accepted custom that federal funds for such purposes don't have to be repaid since it is a responsibility of the federal government, similar to national defense or welfare payments.

By adding the two reservations to the legislation, we could build the South Dakota project under the guise that we were meeting the federal government's responsibility to the reservations. We'd wrap an Indian blanket around the water problems of the West River residents and, at the same time, assist the tribes. If you forgot about the taxpayers (who would be paying the vast majority of the cost), this would be a "win-win" solution.

And that's what we did. The West River residents and the tribes formed an organization to oversee the project, and the legislation was easily passed. Today, the Mni (pronounced "Mini") Wiconi Rural Water Supply Project is delivering water to meet the needs of West River, the Lower Brule Reservation and portions of the Pine Ridge Reservation.

————

This is not the only time an Indian blanket has been used to solve a western water problem. While this may sound like a rather objectionable practice, what we did with the South Dakota legislation is just a freckle on a flea compared to some of the other actions taken on Indian water issues. For more than 225 years, Indians have come out the losers in almost all conflicts surrounding western water. It's a history of greed, corruption, and dereliction of duty on a very large scale.

Like so many water-related issues, this one begins with western settlement. Although the Supreme Court decided the federal government had a responsibility to protect the welfare of Indians, the U.S. government frequently neglected that responsibility. During the nineteenth and early twentieth centuries, settlers didn't hesitate to usurp the water of American Indians in every corner of the West, and the federal government was a willing participant on behalf of the settlers. To paraphrase former California Senator S.I. Hayakawa's comment about the Panama Canal, the settlers and their friends in the federal government "stole it fair and square."

The foundation for correcting this sorry state of affairs was laid in 1908 with the Supreme Court case of *Winters v. United States*. In the early 1890s, Henry Winter (the "s" was added to his name in a clerical error during the court proceedings) and his neighbors in northern Montana began to divert irrigation water from the Milk River. A few years later, the Fort Belknap tribe built an irrigation system downstream from Mr. Winter. During a drought in 1905, the river was drained of water upstream from the reservation. A gutsy U.S. attorney sued on behalf of the tribe, claiming that the tribe had senior rights to the water and Mr. Winter and his neighbors couldn't take the tribe's water.

A federal judge and the Supreme Court found on behalf of the tribe. Their reasoning was that the tribe possessed sovereignty and real property rights in their aboriginal territory long before any treaties with the United States were approved and long before any settlement by non-Indians. At the time that they signed treaties with the federal government, the tribe reserved the right to the water flowing through the lands they historically occupied.

The tribes possessed a reserved water right, under federal law, dating to the year their reservation was established.

While *Winters* clearly laid out the law, it certainly didn't result in positive benefits for the tribes. *Winters* was common knowledge, but was ignored or circumvented by state and federal officials for the next sixty years. As legal scholar Charles Wilkinson has observed, water developers "detested" any rules outside of their tightly controlled state systems, and state officials effectively read *Winters* out of existence by giving away Indian rights without Indian approval. Wilkinson was right when he noted that federal officials, supposedly bound to act as trustees for Indian rights, were the real villains. "They pushed for federal subsidies for non-Indian projects on Indian rivers and ignored potential Indian projects. There were almost no exceptions."

It wasn't until the 1970s that Indian tribes began to exercise their rights and sue to gain restitution of lost water and rights. Assisted by the Native American Rights Fund and other public interest lawyers, tribes filed a series of lawsuits placing a cloud over the future of western water. State officials cried foul, land developers predicted economic ruin, and irrigated agriculture screamed that *their* water was being stolen.

The Water Nobility was outraged, concerned, and threatened. Suddenly, they weren't in control of the process. The law was settled, and it was clear. Tribes had senior rights to much of the water developed in the West. Once presented with the facts, the courts handed the Indians a steady stream of legal victories. The Indians were winning, and for once the Water Nobility was getting the short end of the stick.

But the Indians had problems as well. They couldn't expect the return of their water from major cities across the West like Phoenix, Santa Fe, Los Angeles, Albuquerque, Spokane, and Boise. And tribes weren't planning to go into irrigated agriculture in any major way. By the 1980s, it was clear that operating gaming casinos was much more profitable than agriculture. Finally, lawsuits were long and expensive propositions, and there was always the chance they could suffer a setback from an unsympathetic federal judge.

The solution for the federal government was to promote settlement negotiations between the federal government, the tribes, and state and local interests. The final product would be consummated in a legislative package passed by Congress. In most cases, this is a no-brainer. Members of Congress love a parade, and that is what a settlement is, especially one that avoids a protracted lawsuit and lifts the cloud of ownership surrounding water.

While commendable, these settlements also represented something else: They handed the Water Nobility a fresh opportunity to build the unbuildable and plunder the treasury.

———

Former Secretary of the Interior, Cecil Andrus, once described a particularly objectionable water project as a "dog." The Animas–La Plata Project fits that description.

The Animas and La Plata Rivers run parallel to one another in southwestern Colorado. The rivers run across the Southern Ute Indian Reservation in their southerly journey to merge with the San Juan River in New Mexico. The Animas River is higher in elevation and has flows nearly thirteen times greater than the La Plata River, which lies some ten miles to the west. Because most of the irrigable land lies near the La Plata, irrigators have dreamed of lifting water some 250 feet out of the Animas River and letting it flow toward the La Plata through irrigated fields of alfalfa and pinto beans operated by primarily non-Indians who live in the area. The Southern Ute Reservation has "checkerboard" ownership, meaning Indians and non-Indians alike live within the reservation boundary.

This project was first proposed nearly a hundred years ago and had been kept alive by a series of dreamers and their lawyers and lobbyists who wanted to make it a reality. The project was initially authorized in 1968, but it soon ran into a big problem—it was very expensive and provided few benefits. The costs soared in the 1970s to several hundred million dollars with virtually no benefits to the public. Worse, the project exacerbated the recovery of several endangered species in the Animas River.

Even a Congress that is pretty good about holding its nose and funding some rancid pork wasn't about to touch the Animas–LaPlata Project. Throughout the 1970s, '80s, and early '90s, Congress refused to approve the project.

While the project was stalled, one man, Sam Maynes, kept it alive. Mr. Maynes was an intense and determined Durango attorney. His short stature and western garb (which always seemed to include a magnificent bolo tie) gave him the appearance of being a cowboy, country-bumpkin lawyer. He wasn't. He was a sly, clever, and intense advocate who worked for forty years to make the Animas–La Plata Project a reality.

Maynes, who died in 2004, corralled all the water legal business in southwestern Colorado. He was simultaneously the water lawyer for the Southwestern Water Conservancy District, the Animas–La Plata Water Conservation District, five other water districts, the Southern Ute Indian tribe, La Plata Electric, and the Pittsburg and Midway Coal Company. He also owned the Durango office building that housed his law firm, the Bureau of Reclamation field office, and the Southwestern and Animas–La Plata Water Conservancy districts.

When the 1968 version of the Animas–LaPlata project got into trouble, Maynes helped revive it with an "environmentally positive" alternative. When that alternative couldn't pass muster, he used his position as a counsel to the Southern Utes to propose the project as a means of helping to settle a water rights lawsuit the tribe had filed.

Hiring former Colorado Congressman Ray Kogovsek to assist with the lobbying, Maynes and the local water district now joined with the tribe to secure passage of settlement legislation that would include construction of the project. Throughout the 1990s, they had a willing champion in Ben Nighthorse Campbell, a Native American who represented the area in Congress and later served two terms in the U.S. Senate from Colorado.

Their efforts succeeded in 2000 when the Animas–La Plata Project was authorized for construction as a key component of Indian water rights settlement legislation. The project is an economic and environmental disaster. When Congress finally approved the project, it was estimated to cost over $300 million. The costs ultimately soared north of $550 million.

Even worse, there is no market for the water in the reservoir. None. The water just sits there, evaporating into the atmosphere. To add insult to injury, no recreation is allowed on the lake because the state, federal, and tribal agencies won't provide the facilities. The dam and reservoir it created, according to experts in the state and federal governments, flooded the prime winter habitat for elk and mule deer. The water sits behind the dam waiting for the day when the tribe will be able to sell the water to downstream users such as Phoenix, Las Vegas, or Los Angeles. The tribe sees the reservoir as their next revenue stream to replace oil and gas as those resources are exploited and pumped out. Given the extended drought in the Colorado River Basin, the sale date is fast approaching. For now, it's a hydrologic ghost town and another ecological disaster.

This embarrassing state of affairs was created by wrapping a bad idea in an Indian blanket and handing the bill to the federal taxpayers.

If you look off to the west as you fly into Phoenix, Arizona, you'll see a shiny ribbon of water purposefully winding its way toward the city from the Colorado River. The ribbon is actually the main supply canal for the Central Arizona Project, and it has been the dream of every Arizona politician.

If you were a city developer looking for a place to locate a city of 4.3 million people, the last place you'd pick is Phoenix. It's a hot, arid climate with very little water. After taking control of the Salt

River from the local Indians, early Arizona settlers realized that they still had a problem. There was insufficient ground and surface water to meet the needs of a growing urban population and water-intensive agricultural crops like cotton.

The solution lay three hundred miles to the west with the Colorado River. If a canal could be built to bring Arizona's entitlement from the river, Arizona's future would be guaranteed. This was a simple solution, but a challenging political effort. After more than fifty-five years of lobbying, Arizona got its wish with the authorization of the Central Arizona Project in 1968. Four billion dollars and nearly twenty years later, the project began to deliver water to Phoenix and Tucson.

There was only one problem. During the twenty years it took to construct the project, the local tribes who had had their water stolen many years before filed lawsuits demanding the return of their water. In addition, the tribes had opened successful gaming operations as well as other business and real estate ventures. They were no longer the downtrodden, uneducated Indians who had been pushed aside by early settlers and federal bureaucrats. They were successful businessmen and women, and they weren't about to be pushed around.

The latest effort to resolve the water claims by local tribes is the Arizona Water Settlement Act passed by Congress in 2004. In the annals of water legislation, this settlement will go down as the most breathtaking raid on the treasury ever perpetrated by the Water Nobility.

What does the legislation do? In the simplest of terms, Arizonans picked our pockets for a minimum of $2 billion. The federal government built the state of Arizona a $4 billion project and agreed to have only $2 billion of the costs repaid. That was generous, but as a result of the settlement legislation, both Indian and non-Indian Arizonans got an even better deal.

The legislation requires the $2 billion in repayment to be deposited in a special fund in the U.S. Treasury where the money is reserved for Arizona's exclusive use. The Arizona legislators used an Indian water rights settlement to convince Congress to take $2 billion that should have gone to the treasury, and reserve it for their exclusive use. They created their own slush fund—their own pot of gold.

Even worse, Congress will not revisit this issue on a yearly basis since the legislation provides that the money can be spent from this fund without further action by congressional committees.

The Gila River Indian Community and other tribes who benefit from the legislation certainly came out on top. The tribes have become the new water czars of Arizona. They will ultimately control one-half of the water moving through the Central Arizona Project, and they will be able to use their water for farming or lease or exchange it to local cities for periods up to one hundred years. As trustee, the federal government is required to make this water available to the tribes at no cost.

The potential payoff to the tribes from water leasing to cities is huge. With over 600,000 acre-feet of water potentially available for leasing, it's not hard to see how the Gila River and other tribes will become very wealthy by leasing water—at federal taxpayer's expense. By 2011, the Gila River Indian community had entered into leases with the cities of Goodyear, Peoria, Phoenix, and Scottsdale, and exchange agreements with Chandler and Mesa.

There is a certain ironic justice in this state of affairs since the non-Indians, with the tacit support of federal bureaucrats, originally took the water from the tribes. But it is difficult to understand why we and our children, grandchildren, and even great-grandchildren should have to pay for the greed and incompetence of settlers and bureaucrats who died decades ago.

Incidentally, the largesse gained by the Gila River and other tribes under the 2004 legislation wasn't obtained by happenstance. According to the *Arizona Republic,* between 1996 and 2004, the Gila River Indian community spent more on lobbying in Washington, D.C. than "virtually any other state, city, or tribal government in the nation." In this case, the tribe hired the Washington law firm of Akin Gump Strauss Hauer & Feld (who also represents ExxonMobil, AT&T, and Boeing) and paid the law firm more than $9.16 million to work on the legislation. (When the *Arizona Republic* wrote this article, they weren't aware of the tens of millions of dollars in lobbying fees charged by Jack Abramoff to other Indian tribes.)

The big losers in this legislation are the federal taxpayers. We built a water project for $4 billion and agreed to accept only $2 billion in repayment. This legislation guarantees we won't get that $2 billion, and even worse, we'll pay to make water available to the tribes who can then lease it for hundreds of millions of dollars in hundred-year increments.

Once again, wrapping a water project in an Indian blanket turns out to be a bad idea, and the federal taxpayers have been handed the bill.

Negotiated settlements are the right approach for resolving Indian water rights disputes. There is no doubt that water was taken from many tribes in times past, and negotiated settlements are the best way to correct a bad situation. But Congress should resist efforts to use settlement legislation as a way to build uneconomic or environmentally disastrous water projects or fleece the taxpayers.

This wouldn't be hard for Congress to do. Whenever anyone comes forward with "settlement legislation," the first thing legislators should do is put on the brakes. Any settlement legislation should be carefully considered, thoroughly scrutinized, and it should be exposed to the bright light of public opinion. Congress knows the difference between right and wrong, and they know when an Indian blanket is being used to pull the wool over our eyes.

9

Math Can't Hurt You

*We need to invest in the best science and most accurate
factual information possible to solve water problems.*

When I became commissioner of the Bureau of Reclamation, I
wanted to reform the agency by encouraging the abandonment of
our dam-building fixation. One symbolic way to make that change
was to abandon our involvement in the Three Gorges Dam project
in China.

The Bureau had been advising the Chinese on construction
activities at Three Gorges for many years. I decided early on that I
wanted to terminate our involvement with the project.

Chinese officials conceived the project nearly a century ago.
Throughout the twentieth century, despite wars, famine, revolution, and other interruptions, Chinese officials of all political
stripes doggedly worked to move the project forward. By the early
1990s, the project was finally underway.

There is nothing small about Three Gorges. It is the largest
hydroelectric dam in the world. The installed generating capacity
of Three Gorges is 18,000 megawatts, or three times larger than
Grand Coulee Dam, our largest hydroelectric project. The dam itself spans nearly a mile and one-half across, and towers six hundred
feet above, the world's third longest river. The reservoir stretches
over four hundred miles (longer than Lake Superior), and its construction forced the displacement of more than 1.4 million people.
Construction began in 1994, and the entire project was completed

in 2006, with the reservoir reaching its full height two years later after submerging 13 cities, 140 towns, and 1,350 villages.

With a go-ahead from the Secretary of the Interior, Bruce Babbitt, I quickly announced our withdrawal from the project, and the Chinese were furious. They had their hands full quashing internal opposition to the project, and I wasn't helping out. Given the Chinese reaction, the State Department suggested that I meet with the Chinese to "discuss" the matter.

So I traveled to Beijing and sat in the conference room of the Department of Water Resources, listening to a Chinese official give me a "dressing down" for unilaterally violating an agreement signed by the two governments nearly a decade earlier.

This had been a very formal meeting. The Chinese officials were dressed in matching dark suits and white shirts (reminding me of the movie *Men in Black* without the sunglasses) and speaking through an interpreter with every exchange. The lead Chinese official droned on in a very formal tone, stopping occasionally to let the translator tell me what he was saying.

After nearly three hours of this, the Chinese official concluded his monologue, and the meeting ended. As we rose from our seats and shook hands, he said with a perfect American accent, "Well, that's it for the formal part. How about we go to lunch?" It turns out that he had spent nearly a decade in the United States and had been educated at the University of California at Berkeley. The name of the restaurant where we ate? Three Gorges Restaurant.

After lunch we resumed the meeting and I asked my Chinese counterpart what he considered their biggest water resource problem. His answer was surprising. "Dam safety," he said.

Many dams in China were built during the Cultural Revolution of the 1960s, and they weren't built according to accepted engineering standards. A dam is not just a pile of rocks and dirt. It must be carefully designed, anchored properly, adequately drained, and designed to carry certain loads. Many of the dams built during that period were simply ordered by political functionaries with no consideration for engineering principles. When the functionary ordered a dam built, people started dumping dirt—no plans, no geologic investigations, no engineering analysis, and certainly no environmental studies.

The dams built in China during the 1960s are time bombs waiting to go off. Unfortunately, those who will suffer won't be the "revolutionaries" who ordered the dams. The Chinese water officials of today and tomorrow will be blamed for any mishap, and thousands of people downstream could be drowned.

The blind ambition of some American dam promoters falls into the same category as China's cultural revolutionaries and the dogged promoters of the Three Gorges Dam. They are focused on the end result and don't want to be told that it won't work. Both are spurred on by ideology more than common sense, fiscal responsibility, or engineering practices. The end justifies the means, no matter what the cost.

———

"We are biologists and computer scientists, and what we do is just math. Math can't hurt you."

With those words in November 2005, Michele DeHart, a fish biologist accustomed to working in the background of policy debates, defended her obscure government agency, the Fish Passage Center, against an attack by a U.S. senator determined to put her out of business.

What was all the fuss about? Counting·fish. Who could imagine that counting fish would be controversial?

The dams built by the federal government on the Columbia and Snake Rivers turned once raging rivers into a series of lakes stair-stepping their way out of Canada and Idaho, across Washington and Oregon to the Pacific Ocean. These rivers were once the home of a magnificent salmon fishery. Not any longer. The dams have long since prevented most adult salmon from moving up the river to spawn, and the few offspring that do hatch must migrate through the dams to go out to sea to reach adulthood and begin the cycle again.

Today, several salmon species have been designated as endangered, and federal agencies are charged with doing everything possible to restore them. This restoration process is where the Water Nobility came face to face with the fish counters.

The issue is simple. Fish restoration advocates want the dam managers to spill water in the spring and summer to aid the outmigration of young salmon. This practice results in lost revenue for hydroelectric power and less irrigation water available each summer. But to fish advocates and the scientific community, this approach is the best solution available to restore salmon runs.

The Fish Passage Center is a small agency with only a dozen employees and a budget of less than $2 million. They are responsible for counting the number of fish coming and going at the dams along the Columbia and Snake Rivers. This isn't as easy as it sounds, and it is a very important task. Fish numbers are essential to understand the severity of the fish decline and provide the foundation for solutions.

When the center counted fewer and fewer fish in 2003 and 2004, farmers and customers using power generated at hydroelectric dams began to cry foul. "Something must be wrong," they said, "the numbers are too low." They wanted higher numbers to validate the current restoration approach that they support which doesn't involve spilling water. If things weren't working right, they knew the root of the problem—the people doing the counting must be biased.

The solution of farmers and power users was to go after the messenger, not the message. They found a willing supporter in former Idaho Senator Larry Craig, who decided to abolish the fish counting agency by eliminating its funding in the fall of 2005. The reason? "Data cloaked in advocacy create confusion," Craig said. "False science leads people to false choices."

The response from the Fish Passage Center's director was poignant. "I have never met the man," Michele DeHart, a fish biologist for more than twenty years, said of Senator Craig. "Never talked to him. No one from his office ever contacted us. I guess I am flabbergasted." She then uttered her "math can't hurt you" observation.

The controversy is not a mundane mathematical issue. The dams on the Columbia and Snake Rivers supply electric power to four out of five households in the Pacific Northwest, and the decision to spill water can be expensive. The Water Nobility and the hydropower community don't want water spilled, and they don't like facts that contradict their preconceived notions of how water systems should be operated.

Although the Fish Passage Center is still in business, I'm sure its employees are awaiting the next attempt to put them out of business for simply doing their job.

The Obama Administration came into office with a flurry of activity designed to address the scientific integrity abuses of the Bush Administration. President Bush and Vice President Cheney had been notorious for debunking the science surrounding climate change. They made it abundantly clear to each and every federal employee that climate change was not an issue to be mentioned or cited by government agencies. Employees naturally chafed at this "head in the sand" approach and the Obama Administration swept into office saying they would take the blinders and gags off government scientists. Or, at least we thought.

At the Interior Department, Secretary Ken Salazar issued bold proclamations about scientific integrity, and appointed scientific integrity officers in each of the bureaus. He even issued a scientific integrity policy for the entire department. But policies and press releases don't equate to thoughtful action.

The Bureau of Reclamation hired its Scientific Integrity Officer, Paul A. Houser, in April 2011; he was fired less than ten months later. Houser alleged that he lost his job because he raised concerns about the way the Bureau had represented the science behind a plan to remove four hydroelectric dams from a stretch of the Klamath River. The Interior Department declined to say why Houser had been fired. Houser's allegations have since been investigated, but no reinstatement or justifications for the discharge have been forthcoming.

The debate over the Fish Passage Center and Dr. Houser highlights once again the "win at all costs" approach of the Water Nobility toward water debates. Whether our public officials are Republicans or Democrats, they don't like anyone, and especially federal employees, to voice an alternative opinion. They want employees who will agree with what the Water Nobility has decided is the correct course of action even if it doesn't make scientific sense. They chafe at employees who raise problems, challenge assumptions, and insist on solid scientific evidence for proposed actions.

But isn't that what we're paying these employees to do? Don't we want debate and discussion, and a strong scientific basis for solutions to water problems? It doesn't appear that is the case. Rather than present the facts and debate the right approach, our leaders, no matter what their political leanings, have decided what they want to do based on politics, and they're insisting that their scientists agree with them.

This state of affairs shouldn't surprise us. The water development community has been effective over the years because it has focused like a laser on the results they want, regardless of the consequences. When this myopic approach to decision-making prevails, the wrong decisions are made and taxpayers, the environment, or local residents pay the price.

The Teton Dam in Idaho failed in the mid-1970s, killing fourteen people and causing hundreds of millions of dollars in property damage downstream. This Bureau of Reclamation dam should never have been built at this site, but pressure from the water development community to build the facility overwhelmed common sense.

When University of Arizona economics professor, William Martin, questioned the economics of the Central Arizona Project, he was denied merit pay increases and his career stalled. His analysis turned out to be right.

––––––––

Dams are major construction projects requiring years of planning, careful analysis, consideration of all the alternatives, and adherence to accepted engineering and construction protocols. When completed they provide benefits, but they also bring long-term costs. In addition, dams and levees are dangerous enterprises, as the Teton Dam and Hurricane Katrina disasters demonstrate.

Every successful corporation relies on customer feedback to increase sales or profitability of their product or service. Continuous feedback is critical to their success. Sales data alerts executives to changes in customer preference, the success of competitors, or problems with their product or service. Data and information in today's world are critical, and companies have spent billions to develop and analyze information.

In the water world, we seem to have taken another approach. Advocates for specific solutions know the answers they want, but they don't necessarily want to know the truth. To these advocates, data is irrelevant, unless it supports their solution. They want information to support a predetermined outcome. If data or information doesn't support their position then the data is wrong, politically motivated, or the people who developed it are biased. If business leaders used this approach, their companies would be bankrupt in days.

We need to invest in the development of the best science and information possible about water resources so we can make the most intelligent and informed decisions. Like the bumper sticker about funding education says: "If you think education is expensive, try ignorance."

Without utilizing the talents of our best scientists, we are destined to cause more problems than we solve. Without developing the best information possible, we'll make shortsighted decisions that will turn out to be wrong.

Our willingness to ignore science when it comes to water resource decision-making is astonishing. The water arena is filled with people advocating specific solutions without knowing the most fundamental information. In many cases, they're promoting a solution without knowing the problem.

The willingness to promote a solution before having even the most basic information is not that uncommon. When it comes to water, the Water Nobility and our government leaders go about things in a backward fashion. They settle on a solution first and then work backward, defining the problem based on the solution they've chosen. They use this leapfrog approach because they have allowed short-term political agendas to trump science and data gathering. They have the answer (based on politics) and all they want from scientists is validation for their choice. This is a good example of the old phrase, "Don't confuse me with the facts."

We need to end this approach. Our leaders need to end the dangerous practice of allowing politics to trump science. We need to thoroughly understand the problems we're experiencing and then begin to look for alternative approaches for solving those problems. If we don't take this approach, we'll continue to waste billions of taxpayer dollars on schemes that won't work, or worse, endanger our fellow citizens.

In 1995, I organized a float trip down the Colorado River to commemorate the twenty-fifth anniversary of the publication of John McPhee's classic conservation book, *Encounters with the Archdruid.* In this book, McPhee had floated the river with former Bureau of Reclamation Commissioner Floyd Dominy and the environmental activist David Brower. Their animated conversations about the value of the river for power and irrigation or wilderness values had been a fascinating read.

Rather than rehash their discussions, I decided to take another approach. I invited a cross-section of the water community to accompany me so we could debate and discuss the major water issues facing the West and the nation. We had dam builders, preservationists, lobbyists, lawyers, farmers, and government employees.

The float trip was exciting, but the discussions we had along the river will always stay fresh in my mind. They all had a common thread. During each discussion or debate, it became obvious that we had much to learn about how water systems work and how our use of water is affecting the natural world. Despite building dams for over two hundred years, we seem to know precious little about the impact these dams have on the rivers they block, the fish that inhabit those rivers, and the plants and animals that rely on the rivers. We are, according to one participant, operating in the dark when it comes to the interplay between the science of dams and the natural world.

Because water is developed and distributed primarily by government agencies, we must look to government scientists to provide us with answers to these and other questions about water issues. Unfortunately, in recent years an atmosphere of contempt has developed for those who do science for federal agencies. There is greater demand for scientists to stay within certain political boundaries and not stray into the controversial.

We shouldn't lay blame for this solely at the doorstep of the Bush or Obama Administrations. The pressure to come up with the "right" results started long before either man became President. But both administrations have acquiesced to the Water Nobility and initiated a code of silence from government scientists about water issues.

A political climate that attempts to silence scientists has already had a profound impact on the behavior of government scientists. Because our political leaders are not promoting a culture of inquiry in the water arena and encouraging the pursuit of the unknown, we are forcing many good scientists to leave government service, reach conclusions not justified by data, or remain silent when political leaders mis-characterize their work.

In the spring of 2006, former California Governor Arnold Schwarzenegger proposed a $222 billion infrastructure plan in his State of the State speech that would be kicked off by a $71.5 billion bond-funding package that he wanted approved in the next election. The package immediately ran into a problem over the funding of water projects. Both Republican and Democratic legislators offered up their choices for dam projects totaling several billion dollars.

Only one problem: the California Department of Water Resources had just released their latest five-year water plan and said that the last thing California needed was more dams and surface water storage.

For nearly thirty years, California has undertaken a thorough review of its anticipated water needs and how to address them. In the 2006 version, which was unveiled just before the bond issue debates, the state recommended a fundamental shift in meeting future needs. The authors recommended a broader set of approaches and financing methods. They first recommended investing in urban water use efficiency, then conjunctive management of ground and surface water, promoting recycled water and a host of other approaches. At the bottom of their list of recommendations were investments in surface storage.

The debate between state legislators and the governor's aides reached a passionate level, causing the governor to remark, "This is an issue that almost became a religious issue. It's amazing. It was like the holy war in some ways."

Here were the political leaders of California leading a crusade for their particular dam and reservoir, while their experts were telling them that's the last thing the state should be doing to meet its future water needs. In this case, good sense prevailed for the wrong reason. The legislators couldn't reach an agreement, so the bond package went forward without a water component.

Dam proponents are a persistent group, especially when it comes to developing wish lists of dam projects. After the 2006 debacle, dam proponents came back in 2011 with an $11 billion financing package, but that crashed and burned as well when it became obvious that the voters would reject it. In 2014, California voters approved a "slimmed down" package of water initiatives totaling $7.5 billion. Dam construction funding in the initiative totals $2.7 billion, a mere shadow of earlier proposals. But the projects proposed to be funded by the newly approved bond issue are, according to one opponent, ushering in a new era of big dams including a number of dam projects that had been abandoned because of "low water yield and financial infeasibility ..." Critics labeled the package a "hog fest" of projects unrelated to water supply or drought relief. Even worse, the time required to plan, permit, and construct these projects could take decades, thus guaranteeing that they won't have any impact on California's current water supply challenges.

Has California learned anything from these funding fights? Not much. They do have a comprehensive water plan that is updated on a regular basis, and the plan correctly points out the challenges they face and the need for a comprehensive approach that relies on a mix of solutions. But the siren song of spending public money on dam projects is just too difficult for the Water Nobility to ignore. They cling to the hope—no matter how tenuous—that they can convince the voters to give them billions of dollars so they can spend it to construct large dam projects.

We can have more informed and thoughtful debates if we hire the best scientists and experts and let them seek answers without our interference. We should provide them with a clear statement of what we want to accomplish and when. Then we should get out of the way and let them do their jobs. After they've done their jobs, we will have ample time to debate the alternatives and chart a course forward.

We can invest in science and facts, or we can try ignorance; the choice is ours.

10

Taking Off the Dunce Cap

*We need to encourage solutions to water problems
using innovative, low-cost solutions that promote
conservation and more efficient use of water.*

A dust cloud engulfed the twin-engine plane as we came to a stop on the dirt airstrip on the Pine Ridge Indian Reservation. I was accompanying South Dakota's two senators on an inspection of a makeshift effort that the Bureau of Reclamation employees had undertaken to solve a critical water supply problem.

A portion of the Pine Ridge Reservation had no drinkable water. None. The streams and groundwater in the area were contaminated and some tribal members were forced to walk or drive miles to a community well for their water. This portion of the reservation was located several hundred miles southwest of the area served by the Mni Wiconi Project. The local Bureau staff had proposed an innovative, inexpensive, and controversial solution to this problem, and the senators and I were there to inspect it first-hand.

Bureau employees had first purchased several hundred garbage cans and provided two to each household where there was a drinking water problem. Yes, that's right, garbage cans. Using a surplus government tanker truck that the Bureau had available, tribal employees trucked water from the community well to each household and stored it in the cans. The next step was to design and construct a pipeline using commercially available plastic pipe along the road right-of-way to deliver water from the community well to each household. As houses were hooked up to the pipeline, the interim deliveries would be stopped.

A simple, inexpensive solution to a problem that had plagued the reservation for decades.

When told of the plan, the Indian Health Service opposed it. They were responsible for providing drinking water supplies on Indian reservations, and they didn't want another federal agency invading their territory. It didn't matter that they hadn't managed to solve the problem in the last 125 years. The Bureau of Indian Affairs also opposed the effort, but it was difficult to know why. The best anyone could determine was that since they didn't think of the idea, they were against it.

Despite these recalcitrant federal bureaucracies, the program was implemented, and with the support of the two senators, it delivers water to fifteen hundred people today.

I've always admired the simplicity of this solution. I certainly don't advocate that we run out and buy garbage cans and tanker trucks to meet our future water needs. However, this example shows something rare in the water world: Federal employees who decided to develop a low-cost solution to a water problem without pouring concrete or making a raid on the federal treasury. When addressing water problems, our fixation with building monuments or choosing the elaborate over the simple always seems to prevail. In this case, we chose another path.

But the garbage can example shows us much more. It demonstrates the difficulty that water professionals have in changing the way they approach solutions to problems. They are unwilling to try innovative approaches to problem solving. In this example, the Indian Health Service and Bureau of Indian Affairs would rather leave fifteen hundred people without potable water than change the way they had been going about "solving" the problem.

The unwillingness to change and be innovative has been a

sad characteristic of water professionals for decades. We've sent men to the moon, invented the Internet, and put cell phones in the hands of billions of people. We can get cash on any street corner in the world because of ATMs and our electronic ingenuity and interconnectedness. We have invented countless labor-saving and time-saving processes, new analytical techniques, and a host of new ways for solving various problems. We are an innovative and creative people, except when it comes to water.

When it comes to water, for some reason, we put on a dunce cap. We have little history of innovation, little history of experimentation. We run out the same old solutions year after year, decade after decade. We don't experiment; we don't test the limits.

If there's a flood, how do our experts propose to handle the problem? Their first response is to build a levee to protect populated areas. But we've been doing that for centuries and it doesn't seem to be working very well, as the catastrophe with Hurricane Katrina in New Orleans so sadly showed. Why aren't we looking for new and innovative ways to address this problem? Why are we so stuck in the past?

If we want more water to supply future needs, what's the approach suggested by our experts and politicians? Build a dam and reservoir. Certainly, they think, surface storage and distribution is the best way to meet these needs. Why? We have numerous alternatives to address future water needs. We have amazing computing power at our fingertips, and we can analyze problems in ways we couldn't imagine just five years ago. Do we apply these new analytical techniques? Do we look for new and innovative ways to solve problems?

Unfortunately, we usually don't.

It is true that the old ways work in many cases. The Roman aqueducts have been moving water for thousands of years. The irrigation systems used by the Indians in northern New Mexico before the Spaniards arrived still provide water to local residents.

But imagine what we could accomplish if we developed innovative approaches to today's water problems.

———

Being innovative and willing to try new approaches won't do us much good unless we begin to approach water problems in the right way. The most fundamental change we need to make is to thoroughly understand how we can use the water we have already available most effectively. Only after we make the most of what we have should we look to develop new sources of water.

For hundreds of years we have focused our attention on the supply side of the equation. If we need more water, the logical next step has been to go out and find water that someone else isn't using and deliver it to another location. But that approach isn't going to work any longer.

This realization is slowly beginning to dawn on many water professionals. The member agencies of the Metropolitan Water District ("Met") serve two-thirds of the twenty-seven million people in Southern California. The general manager of Met, Jeffrey Kightlinger, observed in 2006 that, "We've come to realize over the last decade that we're not building new dams, new aqueducts, and moving more rivers to Southern California. We're creating the equivalent of a new river by conservation, water storage, and paying transfer fees" to move water around the state.

Mr. Kightlinger's comment was a significant break with the past. The primary role of the Met's general manager for decades had been to be the cheerleader for damming Northern California rivers and sending the water south or taking more water out of the Colorado River and sending it west to Los Angeles. The Met's fixation for solving its problems by looking hundreds of miles to the north or east has influenced the water politics and policies of the West, particularly California, for the past fifty years.

Despite this pronouncement, the Met is still a powerful supporter of new dams, storage projects, and conveyance facilities, especially when they're built with federal funds. But water conservation is at least in their vocabulary and becoming a viable alternative. Mr. Kightlinger's shift was an important change in the formerly solid wall of opposition to promoting water conservation and the efficient use of water.

Water conservation offers the cheapest, fastest, and most effective approach for addressing our future water needs. Peter Gleick, a noted water expert, has correctly pointed out that, "Water conservation and efficiency are the greatest untapped sources of water in this nation."

The population numbers facing most western communities are so overwhelming that we need immediate answers to ensure that these communities' future needs are met. Building large storage projects and the necessary delivery canals simply will take too much time, cost too much money, and encounter too much opposition to be effective solutions. Water conservation and efficiency are the only legitimate approaches we have for addressing these challenging population numbers.

For nearly forty years, I have tried to promote conservation as one way to solve our water problems. But water conservation is still the exception, not the rule. It is an afterthought, an asterisk. My years of working on water issues have led me to an even more perplexing conclusion about water conservation: There is often a genuine *fear* of water conservation and sometimes *animosity* from the general public, policymakers, and even from professionals in the field toward those who advocate water conservation solutions. Water conservation is just plain annoying to these people.

The opposition of civil engineers who want to build large dams is understandable. They're looking to build a "monument" to demonstrate their professional acumen. But it isn't the engineers who perplex me the most. Water conservation generates a surprising level of emotion, distrust, and even hostility among government administrators, politicians, lawyers, and the press.

Why is it that a sensible, low-cost approach to immediately

impact or solve water problems generates this kind of reaction? Why does water conservation cause almost a visceral reaction against those who promote such solutions?

It may be that people have difficulty visualizing how a water conservation initiative can solve a problem. A dam is a highly visible solution to a problem, a toilet rebate program isn't.

Since most water conservation approaches necessitate people doing things in a different way, some people view conservation mandates as an intrusion on their personal space. Most people in the United States are members of the "leave us alone" coalition, and mandating changes in the way we use water invades that space.

Water has been considered a "free" commodity, and when we increase the price to promote conservation, people are not pleased. Many view this as a form of tax increase.

The press has been unkind to conservation. For some reason, the Fourth Estate seems convinced that water conservation is something only promoted by Hollywood liberals, little old ladies in tennis shoes, or eco-zealots.

In the spring of 2006, the *Sacramento Bee* provided an interesting example of this phenomenon. Their editorial staff was commenting on the fight over the governor's infrastructure bond issue and they observed, with respect to water issues, two camps had developed and were fighting one another with religious-like fervor. The two camps were the "Churches of the Hard and Soft Paths": The "Republican Hard Path (conquering Mother Nature with concrete and subsidized dams) and the Democratic Soft Path (no reservoir subsidies and more water conservation, coastal preservation and Birkenstocks)."

The *Bee* had tried to clearly delineate those arguing over an issue using today's political nomenclature. Two camps: one Republican, one Democrat. Two camps with diametrically opposed approaches: one camp advocating dams and concrete, the other water conservation and no subsidies. One group was tough, masculine, and dressed in hard hats; the other was hippies dressed in

Birkenstocks. The unasked question the paper was trying to suggest was, "Who would you trust to solve your water problems?"

Rather than consider conservation a rational and reasonable approach to solving water problems, a major American newspaper characterized it as an unrealistic approach promoted by the Birkenstock crowd.

Fortunately, a growing number of water professionals are now beyond the name-calling stage. In community after community, local water officials are being forced to address real problems on very unreal timeframes. They are beginning, with increasing frequency, to promote water conservation and efficiency solutions as the first step toward meeting their immediate needs.

In California, demographers estimate another seven million people, or two and a half million new households, will be added over the next fifteen years. That's the same as adding the population of modern-day Houston, Philadelphia, Phoenix, and San Diego to the suburban deserts and canyons of Los Angeles, Riverside, and San Bernardino counties.

Where will we get the water to meet the new residents' needs? They're going to find the water in Southern California, not several hundred miles north or east. It will come through using less water, reusing the water they have, and cleaning up water they've polluted. The California water plan lays out the full breadth of approaches, but conservation is a keystone to future efforts.

Southern California has already started down this path. In the last twenty years, per capita urban water use in Southern California has declined, so Los Angeles can boast that its total water consumption has not risen, despite substantial population growth. Most of these reductions came from the use of water-conserving toilets and other household fixtures, smaller lawns and less outdoor water use by both residential and commercial users.

Metropolitan areas across the West have shown a significant

increase in conservation efforts, and the results from each area show that it is working.

In Las Vegas and southern Nevada, average water use per person dropped by 30 percent between 2000 and 2010, while total water use rose only slightly. Water authorities used a wide assortment of carrots, as well as sticks, to get these results. Residents were paid $1.50 per square foot to yank the grass out of their yards because the average square foot of grass requires 73 gallons of water per year. Authorities paid to turn 154 million square feet (about 5.5 square miles, or a sixth of Manhattan) of grass into desert landscape. They hired "water cops" to look for customers that were wasting water, with fines ranging from $80 for a first offense to thousands of dollars for repeat offenders. They also began to charge a realistic price for water by adopting a tiered pricing structure. Residents pay $1.16 per thousand gallons up to a certain point, and for those who use more, the price can quadruple.

The extended drought in Texas has forced communities throughout the state to look at conservation alternatives. San Antonio has offered a wide range of incentives and rebates for large-scale commercial retrofits to save water, and recycled water from waste treatment plants is now used to replenish the San Antonio River and water golf courses, parks, and commercial uses. A free toilet-replacement program has also brought more than 200,000 water-efficient toilets to homes across the city. Their goal is to save 1 billion gallons of water a year. These efforts are working—the city used the same amount of water in 2009 as it did in 1984, even though its population soared by 67 percent during that period.

But efforts to conserve and reduce consumption can be highly variable depending on a host of circumstances, including geography, lifestyle, and cultural influences. Taking California as an example, per capita water consumption varies widely. As the *San Jose Mercury News* noted, "In steamy Sacramento, where half of the homes still don't have water meters, residents use 279 gallons a day per capita—

almost triple the 98 gallons that residents of foggy San Francisco use. Palm Springs, land of big desert lawns and verdant golf courses, gulps down a staggering 736 gallons a day per person, five times as much as residents of San Jose and Los Angeles."

What is the potential of a comprehensive commitment to conservation? We have a real world example we can look to. In Australia, the populated southeast and southwest corners had to endure the "Millennium Drought" from 1995–2012. This drought changed the way the country managed its water resources, prompting massive spending on desalting plants; grey-water recycling, and rebates and other inducements to homeowners to change consumption practices. The result is that water use by Australians is now half that of Californians. Their biggest difference is reduced outdoor water applications, water-conserving toilet operations, and reduction of leaks.

The Pacific Institute, a California-based think tank, has spent several decades investigating water use in our most populous state. Their conclusion is that the "potential for conservation and efficiency improvements in California is so large that even when the expected growth in the state's population and economy is taken into account, no new water supply dams or reservoirs are needed in the coming decades." By their estimate, one-third of California's current urban water use—more than 2.3 million acre-feet—can be saved with existing technology, and 85 percent of that can be saved at costs below what it would cost to tap into new sources of supply.

No matter how you look at the data and information for Southern California and the rest of the nation, you come to the same conclusion. Water conservation is the largest undeveloped source of water in the nation—cheaper, cleaner, and more acceptable than any other source. What do we have to do to take advantage of this tremendous resource?

The first thing we need to do is jettison our infatuation with building monuments. We must accept the notion that the solution to future water problems lies with using the water we have already developed in a more efficient manner. Changing public attitudes and opinions is another prerequisite. As long as the press and other people view water conservation as a solution pushed only by the Birkenstock crowd, we won't make much progress instituting change.

We need to involve the business community in conservation programs to the maximum extent possible. Continuing to operate under the delusion that government directives will make major changes is nonsense. Water isn't a free commodity. It is expensive to develop, transport, and consume. Businesses study their bottom line and have the incentive to adopt new technology or approaches if they save money. Alternative pricing schemes that encourage creative minds to look for cheaper and more efficient ways of using water is sorely needed.

The Johnson Foundation at Wingspread, located in Racine, Wisconsin, recently announced the results of a six-year intensive, solution-oriented look at how to make U.S. freshwater supplies more sustainable and resilient. The foundation specializes in convening diverse groups of people on compelling national issues in an attempt to find innovative, sustainable solutions. In this case, they involved more than six hundred individuals in the effort to examine our water supply systems from top to bottom. One of the central conclusions of this effort was that historically, capital investments in water infrastructure have been heavily subsidized by federal grants and payments, and water rates have not reflected the real cost of water withdrawn from our nation's rivers and streams.

As they correctly pointed out, "This approach to water pricing has conditioned Americans to assume that water delivery and wastewater treatment always will be inexpensive services, which in turn has driven utilities to defer maintenance and upgrades so that rates remain low." With federal funds on the decline, we can no longer afford to cling to the illusion that water and water services are cheap. "It is time," the Johnson Foundation pointed out, "to rethink how we value water and adopt new strategies and tools that institutionalize its true worth."

As we look at an uncertain water future, one thing is clear. Federal agencies will not be able to develop innovative solutions to our pressing water problems, and there is little hope that they will ever be interested in promoting water conservation and efficiency improvements.

While we won't find innovation at the federal level, there is hope. In the past decade, a number of innovative leaders of local water agencies have emerged. These individuals are reshaping the water field by developing new and innovative approaches to problem solving. These local leaders will be the key to our water future because they are the front-line troops in the battles to address impending water problems.

11

The Elephant in the Room

We must recognize and integrate the realities of climate change in our approaches to solving future water problems.

Backpacking has been one of those pursuits I've enjoyed most when sitting in my favorite easy chair. It's always more pleasant to read a good book about someone plodding along a trail or watch a television documentary of camping out under the stars—rough pursuits from the comfort of your favorite chair.

Yet here I was, in the spring of 2004, stumbling over the rocks, making my way down Fiftymile Creek in southern Utah. Bounding down the trail ahead of me was my eldest son, Nick, who was demonstrating the advantages of youth. With a forty-pound pack on my back and lungs full of dust, I was struggling to keep up and beginning to ask myself why I was doing this.

I had joined an excursion sponsored by the Glen Canyon Institute to investigate the side canyons of Lake Powell behind Glen Canyon Dam, or as the Institute likes to call it, "Reservoir" Powell. The side canyons had become accessible because the reservoir had dropped more than 110 feet over the previous five years as the result of a drought and the shortsighted management policies of the Bureau of Reclamation.

The Bureau had bet on rain and lost. When the drought began in 1999, they assumed it would be a one-year event and rainfall would return to normal the following year. As if taking their instructions from the *Mad* magazine character, Alfred E. Neuman, the Bureau said, "What, me worry? Things will get better next year." But things didn't get better. One year of drought turned into two, two into three, and by 2004 there had been five straight years of drought. This had been the worst drought on record.

But there was a silver lining to this bureaucratic bumbling and extended drought. As the reservoir dropped, the magnificent side canyons and other wonders of Glen Canyon emerged from the water for the first time since the 1960s. The institute was giving tours of the areas being "dewatered," and I was on one of the first tours down Fiftymile Creek.

As we plodded down the creek, Nick and I began to see what had been obscured by the construction of Glen Canyon Dam. The walls of the canyon began to soar toward the sky, and the canyon narrowed to less than a few feet at certain points. A new, breathtaking sight greeted us around each bend. At one point, it seemed like we were walking into a giant clam with a shell eighty or a hundred feet tall. This amphitheater was overwhelming to the senses, even though it was eerily cool and silent. Around another bend we entered a narrow slot canyon with sculpted walls rising sixty feet, blocking out the sun and the mountainous surroundings.

There were reminders that this area had been under water for forty years. The reservoir had left white "bathtub rings" along the sandstone canyon walls. But it was also apparent that the rings would soon disappear. Recent rains had covered up the horizontal rings in many places with vertical strips along the walls. A more important sign of rebirth was the vegetation that had quickly taken hold where there was soil, water, and fresh air. Frogs, lizards, dragonflies, and other fauna were returning. This was a once-in-a-lifetime experience, to see an ecosystem return to life after being in a watery grave for nearly forty years.

As our group sat under the stars that evening recounting our adventures, I recall one member of our group saying, "It's sad that this will be flooded again when we get out of this drought." Everyone nodded silently, and we quickly changed the subject. After being overwhelmed with the beauty of this canyon, no one in our group wanted to talk about how this wondrous place would be destroyed again.

————

Our reticence that night was based on our assumption that the previous five years had been "abnormal" and the reservoir would refill when things returned to "normal." This was the prevailing view of water professionals and advocates. Something had gone "wrong," but nature would get back to "normal" in short order. Those of us sitting in Fiftymile Creek thought like everyone else that Lake Powell had been drained by a drought, but it would refill.

But it hasn't.

As we now know, in 2004 the Colorado River Basin was in the fifth year of a fifteen-year drought, and no one knows how long these drought conditions will continue. But I do know that Lake Powell will not refill in my lifetime, and certainly not that of my children's. Fiftymile Canyon and the many other areas unveiled by the megadrought are now available to be re-discovered.

Glen Canyon isn't the only part of our western water system impacted by the megadrought and the significant re-adjustment of rain patterns. There is growing scientific evidence that the entire premise on which we've built our water supply system is undergoing a radical change. This change is being driven by climate change and portends a very significant restructuring of how we deliver future water supplies.

When I first considered writing this book, I wanted to avoid getting pulled into the debate over climate change and global warming. I wanted to write a book about how the Water Nobility was picking our pocket for billions of dollars and why we needed to address that issue.

The debate over climate change had started out with a somewhat strident tone. The environmental community often seemed shrill in their efforts to alert us to the problems, and at times, their message took on an almost religious fervor. You were either with them or against them. You were either a believer or a heretic.

The Bush Administration and their allies in the conservative community were even worse. They remind me of ostriches sticking their heads in the sand, hoping the problem would go away. Their efforts to avoid coming to terms with the issue of climate change would have been comical if the matter weren't so serious. They browbeat and threatened scientists who reached conclusions that they opposed. They ridiculed or used mean-spirited attacks against those who disagreed with them.

But the debate surrounding climate change and water resource management has matured. Now we have a President that openly embraces the challenge and has offered serious proposals to address climate change. Even the Interior Department now recognizes that climate change is not a problem that we can leave to future generations to solve. In a 2014 report it noted, "Acting now is an economic imperative as well as an environmental necessity."

This is an important turnaround for the Interior Department. Ten years ago, water was considered to be just one of many things that might possibly be impacted by climate change. The implications were not well understood, and there was no consensus. Today, there is agreement about the interrelationship of climate change and water resources, and we now understand that these interrelationships will pose major challenges in the very near future. Our climate is changing, and those changes will have their greatest impact on water resources in the "mid-latitudes of the West" where water availability is largely determined by snow accumulation and runoff. We are experiencing warmer temperatures, and this will shift the timing of spring and summer snowmelt runoff. Water availability will be impacted, especially during summer low-flow periods.

But there are also many things we don't know, and it is difficult to predict with specificity what changes will take place over the next few decades.

Climate change is like an elephant in the room for most of our policy makers, water professionals, and some scientists. Most had denied that climate change was a reality in the hopes that they wouldn't have to deal with it. Now some of them are slowly coming to grips with a new reality.

Climate change is real, and we're going to have to deal with it. If we acknowledge the elephant, it is going to force us to reassess some fundamental precepts of how we've managed water in the past. The first place to begin that reassessment is in how we think about future climate conditions.

What will future climatic conditions be? Should we anticipate more rain or less? What assumptions should we make about when and where rainfall will occur? What are our assumptions about soil moisture, snowfall, evaporation rates, and a host of other factors? We need to make thoughtful assumptions about future climate conditions, interpret information, model future scenarios, and grapple with alternative choices.

Surprisingly, the assumption that climate conditions in the future will not be the same as the past is new thinking. For decades, water professionals assumed that the future would be the same as the past. The past was seen as "normal," and the experts assumed this normal world would exist indefinitely. Nearly all our water supply systems have been designed using this basic assumption.

This fundamental premise of past water planning seems hard to believe. Could our best and brightest engineers and planners have been that myopic? Surely, they didn't just assume that whatever the climate was in the past would be present in the future? Unfortunately, they did.

The entire western water system—all those dams, reservoirs, and canals—were designed and constructed on the premise that the climate that existed in the past would exist in the future. Somehow, we were living in a static unchanging world and this was assumed as normal for design purposes.

This could prove to be a very expensive assumption.

Each year, we ask our water infrastructure to do more. We want more water for endangered species restoration, growing cities, irrigated agriculture, hydroelectric power generation, and other uses. More water, more water, more water. It is becoming increasingly clear that the joint impacts of climate change and future growth demand will make it extremely difficult for our water systems to meet expectations or duplicate past performances.

How severe will this problem be? None of us has a crystal ball, but recent work by scientists is giving us a better sense of what will take place. In its latest study of climate change and California water, the Interior Department predicts that temperatures will rise and rainfall patterns will change. Runoff from precipitation will increase in winter and decrease in spring as more precipitation falls as rain instead of snow. Reservoirs will fill earlier and excess runoff will have to be released earlier to ensure proper flood control. Water demands are expected to increase, especially in urban areas, and water quality will decline. These conclusions mirror those in earlier studies about the potential consequences of climate change on California's water resources.

The implications of these studies can't be over-stated. The practical effect is that the water storage and distribution systems built by the federal government at a cost of tens of billions of dollars will not operate effectively, or could become useless. It is entirely possible, assuming climate change continues, that we will be forced to rebuild or abandon much of the present-day water supply and delivery systems.

————

There is one more consideration that brings some urgency to this situation. The science of "dendrohydrology" is the use of information from tree rings to reconstruct past hydrologic events or trends. By studying the rings, scientists can tell us a great deal about precipitation, evaporation, floods, and droughts that took place hundreds of years ago. If you can find trees growing in the right kinds of habitats sensitive to drought, you can use these trees as a proxy for stream flows back in time. Using this approach, scientists have reconstructed Colorado River flows back as far as 1512.

They've discovered that a good portion of the twentieth century, when most of the water storage facilities were built, was an unusually wet period, probably the wettest period in at least the past five hundred years.

In other words, at least in the Colorado River system, we have built our water supply systems on a faulty premise. We assumed that the rainfall and water availability amounts in the twentieth century were the norm and future conditions would be similar. But the scientific data now indicate that this isn't the case. In fact, the period presumed to be normal was actually an abnormally wet time. Thus, we carved up a water pie, distributed water among various users, and spent billions of dollars on projects to handle an amount of water that likely won't exist in the future.

On the Colorado River, we've always known that we allocated water among the seven basin states using a wet year, and we've struggled to rectify this situation for almost a hundred years. Now, climate change indicates that we may have constructed *most* of our water infrastructure systems based on this faulty assumption as well.

When my former colleagues at government agencies are asked about this issue, they shrug and say, "Yes, it's highly likely we have overbuilt the system and assumed more water than is available." However, they don't want to talk about it, and neither does anyone else.

When California officials updated their statewide plan, they predicted alarming changes in both the near and long-term horizons. They estimate that by 2050, the Sierra Nevada snowpack will decline by one-third, and the sea level in the delta will rise by one foot. These developments will have a significant impact on a system already straining to meet present demands and taxed by increased demand from a variety of water users.

California won't be the only area impacted. In the Columbia River Basin in the Pacific Northwest, modest changes in winter precipitation will result in temperature changes by reducing winter snow accumulation and shifting summer and autumn stream flow to the winter. This will have a significant impact on irrigation deliveries, power production, and endangered species restoration.

In the Colorado River Basin, it is reasonable to assume a 10 percent decrease in average natural flow resulting from climate change. This decrease could result in a 30 percent decrease in hydroelectric generation, violation of salinity standards in the lower river, and significant problems in meeting delivery requirements.

Trying to differentiate fact from fiction and face up to out-of-date assumptions is not easy. But here are some safe conclusions.

Our working assumption that future climate conditions will be the same as the past is dead wrong. It is a faulty assumption, and we need to abandon it immediately. Future climate conditions *will* be different. We can expect warmer temperatures, although it is difficult to predict with great accuracy how much temperatures will increase and where.

In those portions of the country relying on snowmelt for water supply, temperature increases will change the amount of snowpack and timing of snowmelt. We can anticipate less snowpack and earlier runoff.

Our water managers should anticipate less water from the existing system than in the past and less reliable water supplies, as well as less generation of hydroelectric power. There will be greater competition for water supplies as demand grows and our supply systems strain to meet them.

We will need to make better choices about what we do with our limited supplies. There is a critical need to focus on the demand side of the equation (such as water conservation) as a way of relieving the burden on our water systems.

We also need to start making some hard decisions about how we operate our present water systems. Draining Lake Powell and removing Glen Canyon Dam, as I have recommended, is just the beginning of the many hard decisions we will have to make.

It's difficult to anticipate how the Water Nobility will react to the specter of changing climate conditions. However, based on past performance, here's what we might expect. The Water Nobility will likely call for several radical changes in water policies, including: construction of new dams and pipelines; repeal or relaxation of environmental standards (and particularly the Endangered Species Act); or re-allocation of water away from environmental uses to farms. Why wouldn't they? If their past record is any indication, they just might get their way.

Climate change can be an abstract and remote issue, and it seems to be a far-off concern. Surely, we have lots of time to look for answers. What about creating a government commission to study the issue, debate the science, and suggest alternatives? What about more hearings in Congress and debates about the pros and cons of various choices?

The solution to nearly any water issue takes significant lead-time. When you mention infrastructure, it takes years to plan, finance, and construct facilities. Because government funding is involved, we need to have time to debate alternative choices. This is not a system that can turn on a dime. We can't put off decisions until tomorrow. The time to begin to look for solutions is now.

The future management of our water resource systems is going to be more challenging. We cannot continue to ignore the impact of potential climate change on our water systems. We need to acknowledge the range of potential impacts that can occur and begin to seriously integrate climate change alternatives into our decision-making.

———

Thinking back to the discussions we had under the stars during our excursion down Fiftymile Creek, it's obvious to me now that we had it wrong. We assumed "normal" was what the reservoir had been prior to the drought. It now seems easy to predict that what we thought to be normal won't appear again in our lifetime.

In March 2014, Lake Powell was at an elevation of 3,575 feet. It hadn't been this low since Lyndon Johnson was President and Elvis was performing in Las Vegas. None of the experts I've talked with are even discussing the possibility of seeing the reservoir return to its pre-1999 levels. The major debate today is how low the reservoir will drop and how fast.

When the debate took place to authorize the construction of Glen Canyon Dam, there was little if any debate about what was being inundated. Glen Canyon is a beautiful, even magical place. It is a national treasure, and it is a tragedy that it was flooded. It would be an even bigger tragedy to flood it again.

Climate change will force us to reconsider the choices we made in constructing Glen Canyon Dam and many other structures. Given the new climate realities that we know are coming, I hope we can make more intelligent decisions by removing Glen Canyon Dam and making other hard choices to meet an uncertain water future.

12

An Agenda for Reform

As the words "Thank you for giving me the opportunity to speak to you today" left my mouth, I expected a chilly reception. I was wrong. I got a frigid reception; there were a hundred and twenty-five people in the room, and one man was clapping.

It was 1995 and I had accepted an invitation to address the International Committee on Large Dams in Varna, Bulgaria. The United States started the organization after World War II as part of its Cold War strategy. Dam-building was then a tool of diplomacy as the United States and the Soviet Union used every opportunity to joust with one another, including trying to see who could build the most dams in the Third World. The international committee met every two years to persuade themselves that large dams were a good idea.

I had come with one purpose in mind—to tell them the dam-building era in the United States was over. "We no longer can count on public or political support for construction projects," I observed. I predicted that the projects underway would be completed as quickly as possible, but "the opportunity for any future projects were extremely remote, if not nonexistent."

There it was. A clear, forceful, and bold prediction to a room full of dam builders. Their solution to water problems was going to fade away just like the Cold War. The lone delegate from the Netherlands agreed with me because he was clapping enthusiastically. All the other attendees sat silently with their hands on their laps, looking somewhat confused. Here was the head of one of the largest dam-building agencies in the United States telling them that the work they had been doing for their careers, all their dreams, would disappear.

My prediction was bold, and it was wrong.

———

In the twenty years since I made that speech, the pendulum has swung in the other direction. Rather than seeing the demise of big water projects, there have been renewed calls for the construction of large dam and pipeline projects throughout the United States. They are still being pushed by a small group of advocates and being embraced by a willing Congress. The opportunity for new projects isn't "extremely remote" as I predicted in 1995. Big dam projects seem to be gaining traction and getting approved or are being seriously considered with increasing frequency. The Water Nobility is alive and well.

The $25 billion Bay Delta Conservation Plan proposed by California Governor Jerry Brown and the Obama Administration certainly leads the parade of big water proposals. It is an audacious proposal that will send California and U.S. taxpayers an outrageous bill, and put off solving California's water issues for decades. While it's one of the biggest proposals, it certainly isn't the only one.

The Flaming Gorge Pipeline is a proposed private venture calling for a five-hundred-mile water pipeline to pump 250,000 acre-feet of water per year out of the Green River in Wyoming for use along the Front Range of Colorado. This proposal would suck approximately 20 to 30 percent of the river's annual flow, and cost between $7 and $10 billion without including any costs to deal with the massive environmental impacts the pipeline would cause. One organization dubbed it the most expensive water in Colorado history.

State and local officials of Utah are actively working to build the Lake Powell Pipeline project. This proposal calls for pumping 86,000 acre-feet of water out of Lake Powell and running it through a pipeline to St. George, Utah, at a cost of approximately $1.4 to $2.4 billion. St. George was one of America's ten fastest growing cities between 2000 and 2010, and in 2012, it was the second fastest growing metropolitan area in the country. The city is located halfway between Salt Lake City and Las Vegas and has become a retirement Mecca. Unfortunately, it's located in an arid desert valley in the northeastern Mojave Desert and water supplies are limited. Piping water from Lake Powell to St. George is seen as a quick, easy solution to the community's problems, even though it is questionable whether residents could pay for the project and if there is even sufficient water to put into a pipeline.

The Southern Nevada Water Authority has proposed a three-hundred-mile buried pipeline system to convey groundwater from central and eastern Nevada to southern Nevada at a total cost of $15 billion. The water authority has already spent tens of millions of dollars on permitting and prep work for its pipeline and received some of the needed permits and approvals. But a long string of court challenges lie ahead, and the fierce opposition from rural residents, ranchers, Indian tribes, conservationists, outdoor enthusiasts, and even the Mormon Church will have to be overcome.

But the proposals don't stop there. In 2009, Congress quietly authorized two large pipeline projects in New Mexico. The Ute Lake Project will deliver water to rural communities in eastern New Mexico. The project will move a meager 16,500 acre-feet of water for the incredible sum of $550 million, or a cost per acre-foot of $33,400. The Navajo-Gallup Pipeline project will cost over $850 million to deliver 36,000 acre-feet to rural communities and tribes in western New Mexico.

Even more large projects are in the planning stage in the upper Colorado River Basin. The Northern Integrated Supply Project that would take water out of the Cache la Poudre River north of Denver is anticipated to cost anywhere from $500 million to over $1 billion to deliver 40,000 acre-feet of water. The Yampa River Pumpback Project on the Yampa River would move water from the Colorado River drainage to the Front Range of Colorado for a cost in excess of $3 billion.

These and other big projects are being authorized or proposed to meet the individual needs of relatively small geographic or urban areas. They are being treated individually, as one-off projects. But we need to recognize that when taken together, these projects represent a significant new phase in western water policy.

Barry Nelson, with the Natural Resources Defense Council, correctly asked where the water to supply these projects would come from. "In a river that is over-allocated today and projected to be drier in a warmer future, the most likely answer is that the water pumped by large new pipelines would come from those who are using that water today."

These projects are not developing "new water." It's a shell game. These projects are simply taking existing water from other users, and more than likely, those users are unaware of the consequences. And remember, this shell game is taking place in the Colorado River Basin where everyone admits that water supplies are insufficient, and could get much worse even without big projects.

Obviously, grandiose plans and wishful thinking aren't just the purview of federal officials. State governments, urban water districts, and even the private sector are behind each of these multi-billion dollar proposals of questionable merit—paid for by taxpayers.

———

In 1995, the Bureau of Reclamation had been restructured and refocused on environmental priorities, and thoughts of building bigger dam projects were behind them. I sincerely believed the dam-building era in the United States was over. As I told the stunned delegates in Bulgaria, U.S. water policy had changed. Urban residents wanted water left in the river. Federal funds were no longer plentiful and environmentalists were major players in our debates. Most important, I felt that public support for subsidies to a small number of agricultural producers or landowners, who had been the foundation for most of our water decision-making, had waned.

But things haven't worked out that way. While many urban residents, environmentalists, and Indians are now major players in our water debates, a small number of agricultural water districts, farmers, city leaders, and business interests are still driving our water decision-making. They have become the Water Nobility, and they are the driving force behind the water decisions being made across the West and in the halls of Congress.

Members of Congress seem to be unapologetically willing to spend federal funds for every conceivable kind of project to please their constituents. Not even the groundswell of the Tea Party and the government spending reduction advocates that they spawned have been able to turn off the federal-funding spigot. The congressional addiction for earmarks, especially those for water projects, justifies coining a new phrase to describe these projects. "Pork barrel" is simply too meek a phrase to describe a project costing several billion dollars that can't pass a straight-face test when explained to the average voter.

Currently, there seems to be little appetite in our political system for trying to reform water policies. The advocacy community is quiet or disinterested. The Tea Party zealots appear to have lost interest in holding the line on government spending. Reformist members of Congress seem reluctant to speak up about water reform. The overwhelming majority of politicians want to continue to deliver pork to their constituents back home. The congressional leadership has sat idly by while members have gleefully developed new ways to provide earmarks (by another name) or more subsidies to enrich a small number of people.

The few people who do speak out are unwilling to identify and criticize the Water Nobility who are the architects and promoters of our problems. The Water Nobility is the best-kept secret in the water world. They are flying under the radar, and for some reason, they are perceived as a powerful force that must be served or avoided. Their perceived power and influence has caused politicians and advocates alike to cower at the mention of their names, or leap to serve them no matter what they ask. No request seems to be too outrageous. Today, the Water Nobility isn't content with asking for hundreds of millions of dollars—they now want billions.

There is a critical need for the public to become concerned about what is going on. Most people are in the dark about these issues because water issues are, well, boring. When my daughter was a teenager, I took her with me on a field visit of water projects around Reno, Nevada. We toured Lake Tahoe, Pyramid Lake, the Truckee and Carson Rivers, and discussed Indian water rights and endangered species issues with the experts. To me, it was an exciting, even stimulating day. As we ended the tour and the sun was dropping over the Sierra Nevada Mountains, I turned to her and said, "What did you think? Pretty interesting, huh?"

Her reply was honest and ego crushing: "Dad, this has been *the* most boring day of my life."

I will always remember her reply because it was a wake-up call for me. The general public is not interested in the details of water project fights or the nuances of water legislation. It's just too abstract or esoteric or dull.

I suppose that's what goaded me into writing this book. I knew there had to be a good reason why no one else had spoken out on these issues. Despite this reticence, there was a need to trudge ahead. There should be a national outrage over the billions of dollars being spent to finance the lifestyle of an elite group of individuals, and that group wants even more handouts.

The ten basic reforms explained in earlier chapters will help channel that emotional outrage in a productive way, and result in better water policy decisions in the future. Those changes include:

1. We need to stop catering to the Water Nobility, who has secured a grip on western water.
2. The federal government should not subsidize the delivery of water from its projects.

3. The Bureau of Reclamation should be abolished because it is an outdated federal bureaucracy.
4. An independent commission, not Congress, should recommend the individual water projects to be funded each year.
5. We should remove unnecessary and environmentally destructive dams to restore our rivers and streams, and we should begin that effort with Glen Canyon Dam.
6. The federal government should terminate its involvement with the largest irrigation district in California.
7. Settlement of Indian water rights claims should not be used as an excuse to build uneconomic water projects or fleece the taxpayers.
8. We need to invest in the best science and most accurate factual information possible to solve water problems.
9. We need to encourage solutions to water problems using innovative, low-cost solutions that promote conservation and more efficient use of water.
10. We must recognize and integrate the realities of climate change in our approaches to solving future water problems.

If we make these changes, our water policy decision-making will be on much sounder footing. We will make better decisions, and we'll make better use of limited taxpayer dollars. The system won't be perfect, but it will be a dramatic improvement over where we are today.

These reforms will enable us to retake control of water policy from the Water Nobility who has hijacked it from us over the past forty years. Our pocketbooks and our environment shouldn't be under the exclusive control of a small group of people with a narrow, self-serving agenda. We deserve better.

These reforms will enable us to control the insatiable appetite of the members of Congress to use our money to boost their re-election chances, or feather their nest with a narrow group of constituents back home.

These reforms will also guarantee that we approach the future in a more rational manner. Rather than continuing to do what we've done in the past, we will be able to focus on new, innovative solutions that promote more efficient use and conserve the water we presently have.

Water is a necessity of life, but it is also much more. It is critical to our economic future. It provides habitat for fish and other aquatic life. It sustains the world around us. And it provides a source for recreation and play.

Because it is so important, water policy-making and implementation should not be left in the hands of a few people. It belongs to all of us, and we should all have a voice in charting a more thoughtful water future.

Index

DANIEL P. BEARD has been a forceful advocate for reform of water resource policy and management issues for more than four decades. He has extensive experience working in the private sector and government. His government service includes positions with the White House, U.S. Senate, House of Representatives, Interior Department, Library of Congress, and serving as Commissioner of the Bureau of Reclamation. He currently lives in Columbia, Maryland.